TOKYO HAiR

最先端ヘアスタイルストーリー

INTRODUCTION

時代の最先端、感度の高いヘアスタイルが生まれている街はどこだろう。
また、ヘアサロンが世界で一番密集している街はどこだろうか……。
それは"東京"、"TOKYO"である。

そう"TOKYO HAIR"は、世界から最も注目を集めているといっても
過言ではないだろう。

では、そんな"TOKYO HAIR"を牽引してきたヘアサロンはどこだろう？

それは1970年代より川島文夫氏が主宰するPEEK-A-BOOであると
行きついた。

そこで今回warp MAGAZINEの連載でもご縁のあった
PEEK-A-BOOに監修をお願いし、業界関係者はもとより、
感度の高い読者に向けて、切れ味鋭いコンテンツの詰まった
"TOKYO HAIR"を英訳付きで世界に向けて発信する。

The town where the advanced sensitive hairstyle of the times is born
 will be wherever.
In addition, where is the town where hair salons crowd most in the world?
It is "Tokyo", "TOKYO".

Even if it is said that "TOKYO HAIR" attracts attention most from the world,
it will not be exaggeration.

Then where will the hair salon which pulled "TOKYO HAIR" be?

Therefore We asked PEEK-A-BOO connected with each other by serialization
of warp MAGAZINE for the supervision.

When it was PEEK-A-BOO which Fumio Kawashima presided over from
the 1970s, We arrived at it. We add a book to a person concerned with industry,
a reader of the sensitivity and send one of sharp contents for the world.

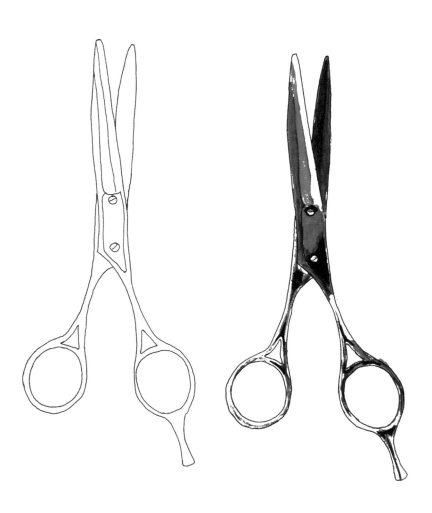

CONTENTS

- 002 INTRODUCTION
- 006 CHAPTER_01 最先端の東京ヘアカタログ
- 038 CHAPTER_02 街中で見かけた髪型の優良サンプルをスナップ
- 060 CHAPTER_03 TOKYO HAIR を創出するヘアスタイリストに密着
- 082 CHAPTER_04 個性際立つ著名人のヘアスタイル
- 094 CHAPTER_05 コシノジュンコ × 川島文夫のヘアスタイル談義
- 100 CHAPTER_06 なりたいヘアスタイルを実現するためのオーダーリスト
- 112 CHAPTER_07 理想のヘアスタイルを作るためのお悩み Q&A
- 122 CHAPTER_08 TOKYO HAIR を支える、7つの神器
- 130 SHOP LIST

Part

I

TOKYO HAIR CATALOG

最先端の東京ヘアカタログ

目まぐるしく変わるヘアスタイルのトレンド。
どうせなら、旬な髪型で他の人と差を付けたいところ。
ここでは、PEEK-A-BOOのスタイリスト西尾卓義氏が手掛けた、
今の東京を象徴するヘアスタイルをご紹介。

Tokyo's freshest hair catalog

Created by PEEK-A-BOO stylist Takuyoshi Nishio;
here are the latest Tokyo hairstyles.

01

Black Halfcarl Short

黒髪とパーマで作る知的なショートスタイル。表面にレイヤーを入れすぎないことで落ち着いた印象に仕上がっている。アレンジでフロントをジェルなどでアップすれば、しっかりとビジネスモードにシフトチェンジが可能。

A black, permed, and sophisticated short style. this less-layered cut can also suit for business scenes when the front is combed back with hair gels.

model:Alberto

Front

Side

Back

Arrange

02

Layer Short

全体のフォルムがひし形の外ハネスタイル。顔の真横にハネる髪を作ると、好バランスが生まれる。束感が出るように握ってスタイリングすればOK。耳に掛けたアレンジで、より大人っぽさをプラスするのもオススメだ。

A balanced rhombic silhouette style. Wax with thicker bundles or tuck the lose ends behind ears for mature look.

model:Daiki

Side

Back

Arrange

Front

03
Ash Beige Short

アクティヴなモードスタイルで、人と差を付けたい人にオススメなのが、ハイトーン＆カールスタイル。アレンジでウェット系ワックスを使用し、毛先から握る様にスタイリングすれば、よりモードさを強調できる。

Hi-toned and curly style for active and stylish look to stand out. Wet texture wax will also add much chic impression.

model:Kei

Side　Back　Arrange

Front

04
Chin Length Bob

あえて切りっぱなしにして毛先に動きを出したワンレングスボブ。メンズの場合は、毛先から中間にパーマは必須。スタイリングはハーフドライの髪の毛先に、ウェットオイルワックスを少量揉み込んで自然乾燥でOK。

A playful uni-length bob. Permed ends needed for men. Set the semi-dried hair with wet texture wax.

model:Yuuki

Side　Back　Arrange　Front

05

Wavy Mush Short

毛先にランダムなウェーブをプラスし、カジュアルな印象に仕上げた現代風マッシュルームカット。甘すぎない程度のやんちゃ感がポイント。柔らかめなワックスを毛先から揉み込むようにスタイリングして整えれば完成。

A mushroom style with modern twist. Styled with soft wax throughly.

model:Shuntaro

Front

Side　Back

Arrange

06

Cheekbones Length Short

ミステリアスな雰囲気漂うモードな前下がりのショートヘア。長さの設定が重要で、頬骨の長さにすれば小顔効果が得られる。さらに、前髪の分け方によって雰囲気をガラッと変えられるのも、このヘアスタイルの特徴だ。

A mode and chic short style. Setting the length right on to the cheek bone for slimmer face line. The style can also give different Impressions by playing with bangs.

model:Takahiro

Front

Side

Back

Arrange

07

New Regent

リーゼントとは"サイドからバックにかけてタイトに流す"スタイルのことで、グリースでしっかりなでつけるようにシェープするのがポイント。フロント部分は、揉み込むように少し高さ&動きを出すのが、旬なリーゼントスタイルだ。

The pompadour up-to-date. Comb with grease firmly and create hight and move in the front.

model:Toshimitsu

Front

Side

Back

Focus

08

Spiky Very Short

男らしい刈り上げスタイル。トップの部分が1番長くなるようにすることで、バランスの良いシルエットが実現。タオルドライ後に、ジェルを付けるだけの楽ちんスタイル。毎朝のセットに手間を掛けたくない方にオススメだ。

Easy, masculine, shaved style with volume on top. Wipe with a towel and apply hair gel then good to go. The best time-saving cut for busy morning.

model:Nariyoshi

Front

Side

Back

Focus

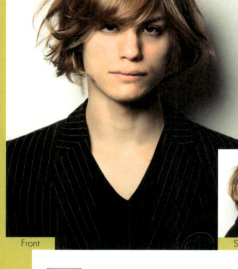

09

Natural Wave × Bob

重めのボブスタイル＋毛先にハーフカールでユニセックスな雰囲気に。直毛の場合は、中間から毛先にゆるくボディパーマをかけることで、オシャレ度がアップする。ミストタイプのワックスでくしゃっと無造作にスタイリング。

Thick bob with slight curl for unisex style. Style with mist-wax for natural finish.

model:Osker

Front　Side　Back　Focus

10

Wavy Short

頭のハチ付近まで刈り上げたツーセクション。フロント部分を少し長めに残しウェーブ感をプラスして、毛流れが印象的な大人っぽい雰囲気に。グリースワックスでウェットな質感にアレンジすればOKな簡単スタイルだ。

A boldly shaved two-section style. Leaving length and volume on front will create sexy mature look. Can be styled easily with wet grease wax.

model:Ryota

Side　Back　Focus　Front

11

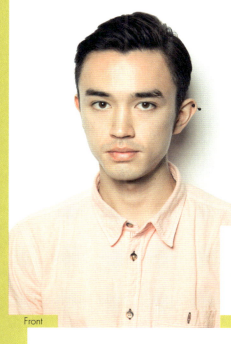

American Ivy

トップからフロントにかけて徐々に毛先を長くカットするのがポイント。スタイリングは、グリースを全体になじませ、コームで7:3分けにスタイリング。清潔感と手入れが簡単なことから、常に人気を呼ぶヘアスタイルだ。

To create the style, cut gradually longer from the top to the front and style with grease. Comb and part the hair in 7 to 3 for clean look.

model:James

Side

Back

Focus

Front

12

Soft Spiky Short

トップに動きを出すため、あえて長さを不揃いにカットしたスタイル。ハードワックスでねじるようにスタイリングすると上手にまとまる。カラーは、ブリーチした後にアッシュベージュをプラスしているのがポイントだ。

Giving a random length for playful top, this style can be completed with twisting hair bundles with hard hair wax. Recommended with bleached then colored in ash beige hair.

model:Takafumi

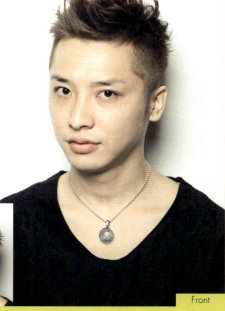

Side

Back

Focus

Front

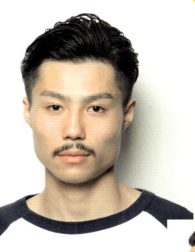

13

Wild 7:3 Hair

ワイルドかつ男らしさのなかに、清潔感があるこのスタイル。ファッションを問わず、ビシッとキマるヘアスタイルだ。スタイリングは、ハーフドライ後にジェルをつけて、手ぐしで7:3パートを作れば簡単に完成する。

A wild, masculine and clean style. For the styling, dry the hair halfway and apply hair gel, then part in 7:3 with hands.

model:Kentaro

Front　　　　　　　　　　Side　　　Back　　　Focus

14

Head Shape

ツーブロックに飽きた人にオススメしたいベーシックなショートスタイル。頭の形に合わせた立体的なフォルムを作ることで、ワイルドな印象と洗練さを合わせ持った雰囲気に。スタイリングは、ワックスをなじませるだけでOK。

A back to basic short style with wild and sophisticated impression. Easily styled by applying hair wax.

model:Ryo

Side　　　Back　　　Focus　　　　　　　　　　Front

15

Two Block × Back Gradation

今や定番スタイルであるツーブロックだが、秋冬のスタイルでは、表面とフロントに長さを残して耳にかけるようなスタイルが◎。アレンジで、フロントを下ろしてもキマる、2WAYとしてもオススメなヘアスタイルだ。

An updated two-section style. Leaving enough length on the front and surface to create different impression when the hair is tucked behind the ears.

model:Isao

Side

Back

Focus

Front

16

Side Gradation

'80年代のスケートシーンで大人気だった、トニー・ホークをイメージ。日本でも様々な時代で見られる定番的なヘアスタイルだ。スタイリングのポイントは、ジェルやワックスを手グシでかき上げるように仕上げたい。

Tony Hawk inspired style. This basic and popular cut can styled with hair gel or wax with hand comb.

model:Takahiro

Side

Back

Focus

Front

17

Nuance Short

ハチから下は甘めな刈り上げでタイトに見せ、トップからレイヤーを入れて軽さをプラスする。量を減らしすぎないのが今っぽいショートヘアのポイント。マットなワックスを少量揉み込んで毛束感を出すようにスタイリング。

A clean shaved neckline with layered top style. The tip is not to thin the hair too much to keep an urban look. Matt texture wax is the best choice for styling.

model:Devin

Side

Back

Focus

Front

18

Wavy Bob

バックからフロントにかけて前下がりのグラデーションを入れて、頭の形を良く見せるボブスタイル。ランダムなウェーブをかけることで、外国人のような雰囲気のクセ毛を表現することができる。

A balanced gradation bob style. Adding random waves can create laid-back and natural curly look.

model:Yu

Side

Back

Focus

Front

| 19

Square Short

サイドからバックにかけてバリカンでラインをしっかり作ることで、ナチュラルなベリーショートにエッジの効いた強さをプラスすることが可能。マットなハードワックスを毛先になじませ、毛流れに合わせて仕上げるだけ。

An edgy shot style for bold look. The horizontal side shave is the key to this style. Apply matt hard wax for the finish.

model:Keita

Front　　　　　　　　　　　　Side　　　　Back　　　Focus

| 20

Curly Short

スラムダンクの宮城リョータを思わせるバリカン＆カーリースタイル。程よく丸いフォルムにすることで、シンプルな夏のＴシャツや、タンクトップに合わせやすいヘアスタイルに。ハーフドライの後にジェルを揉み込めば完成。

Inspired by Ryota Miyagi, a famous character from all-time-favorite "SlamDunk." This shaved and curly style with round silhouette can be finished with hair gel on semi-dried hair.

model:Shohei

Side　　　Back　　　Focus　　　　　　　　　　　Front

21

Minimum Short

バリカンによるサイドからバックにかけてのグラデーションがポイント。フロントが立ち上がるくらいタイトに作り、額を見せた男らしいベリーショート。スタイリングはマットワックスをなじませ、フロントを最後に立ち上げる。

A wild very-shot with length gradation from the side to rear. Style with matt texture wax and give volume in front.

model:Sumihiko

Front　　　　　　　Side　　　　　　Back　　　　　　Focus

22

Two Block Curly

1度はチャレンジしたいハイトーンのカールスタイル。トップにボリュームを持たせてハチから下をタイトに作ることで、ワイルドさと清潔感がミックスできる。パーマはロッドの大きさをランダムにして立体感を強く出そう。

A hi-toned curly style. Volumed top and tight bottom can create wild and clean look. Using different with for perm will give solidity to the hair.

model:Kyohei

Side　　　　Back　　　　Focus　　　　　　　　Front

23

Sleek Short

ツーブロックの設定を低めにし清潔感のあるダウンスタイルに。キレイ目なシャツやジャケットに合わせやすいヘアスタイル。柔らかめのグリースをなじませて荒目のコームでとかし、毛流れをつくるのがポイントだ。

A Longer length two-section for clean look. Create smooth flow with wide-teeth comb and soft grease for styling.

model:Shingo

Front

Side

Back

Focus

24

Crew Cut

カットの際に、アウトラインからハチまでをグラデーションに整える。スタイリングはグリースを付けてからジェルを重ね、ツヤを出して仕上げる。ニームで 8:2 分けにし、オールドスクールな雰囲気をプラスする。

Creating gradation in length from wider part of the skull to the neckline. This style can be finished by 7:3 combing with both grease and gel for polished look.

model:Onoue

Side

Back

Focus

Front

25

Grunge Short

カットの際に、サイドの内側をやや短めにすることがポイント。これにより動きがあり、遊び心のあるショートスタイルが完成する。スタイリングは、あえてツヤを出さずに、バサッとした質感に仕上げるのがオススメ。

The tip for this style is slightly shorten inner layer on the sides, which creates a playful movement. Recommended finish is matt texture.

model:Iccho

26

Two Section Style

頭の形を綺麗に見せるために、アンダーセクションをタイトに切り込み、オーバーセクションを少し長めにしたツーセクションスタイル。ワックスを使用しトップをふんわりさせ、髪を横分けにすることで清潔感がプラスされる。

Formed by tight cut under section and longer top. This style needs volumed wax top and bangs parted to sides.

model:T.

27

Short Ivy

サイドをバリカンでグラデーションにして、全体のフォルムをスクエアに。7:3パートをトリマーで作り、白シャツを合わせることで、清潔感と男らしさを演出する。水性ポマードとジェルをミックスしたスタイリングが◎。

A square-cut silhouette style. Style with mixture of water-soluble pomade and gel for clean look.

model:Shohei

Front　　Side　　Back　　Focus

28

80's Medium

長めの前下りミディアムスタイル。フロントは目に掛かるくらいにして全体に外ハネMIXのパーマをオン。'80年代のアイドルやミュージシャン風のスタイルは、ネルシャツとも好相性。ムースを全体になじませるだけOK。

A permed medium style imagining a 80's pop-star. Easy to style with hair mousse.

model:So

Side　　Back　　Focus　　Front

29

UK Short

トップに動きが出るくらいのレイヤースタイル。カラーは1度トーンアップしたあとにスモーキーなベージュをのせ完成。RADIO HEADのトムヨークのような柔らかく動きのあるスタイルは、アースカラーのシャツと好相性。

A layered short style colored in smoky beige over slightly bleached hair.

model:Yuta

Front

 Side
 Back
 Focus

30

Moving Short

ミュージックビデオや映画など、独特な世界観の作品を手掛けるミシェル・ゴンドリー監督をイメージ。跳ねるようなクセっ毛と甘めに刈り上げたフランス人風スタイル。ウェット感あるスタイリングがマッチする。

A Curly short hair like French director Michel Gondry. Recommended with wet styling.

model:Taku

 Side
 Back
 Arrange

Front

31

Asymmetry

'80〜'90年代にかけてのバンドのドラマーをイメージしたヘアスタイル。硬派なドラマーを変形モヒカンで表現した。フロントセンターをズラすことで、立体的に見せることも可能だ。サイドのラインもポイント。

An asymmetry mohawk as a homage to a 80's to 90's drum player in a music band. Adding side lines also give a character to the hair.

model:Kanata

Side

Back

Focus

Front

32

Very Short

全体のフォルムがスクエアな印象のバリカンスタイルは、男っぽさと強さを演出。サイドからバッグにグラデーションでバリカンを入れて、頭の形をよく見せることも可能。アレンジで大人っぽくクールに見せることも可能だ。

A masculine square short style. The skilled cut can create a balanced head silhouette.

model:Sotaro

Side

Back

Focus

Front

33

Mush Short

少し甘い雰囲気の前下りショートスタイルは、フェイスの形をカバーして、より柔らかい印象にしてくれる。顔まわりのボリュームが欲しかったり、ハードにはしたくない人にオススメ。アレンジでガラリと印象を変えられる点も◎。

This short style will give a soft and gentle impression, but you can also go wild with different hair stylings.

model:Tetta

Front

 Side

 Back

 Arrange

34

Very Short × Carl

ベリーショートは、直毛の人でも毛先をハーフカールさせることで雰囲気を出すことができる。トップの長い部分と刈り上げ部分をあえて繋がらないようにカットするのがポイントだ。冬でもスッキリ見せたい人にオススメ。

This curly short is easy to set. Making a clear transition between Volumed top and tight shaved part gives a character to this style.

model:Eisaku

 Side

 Back

Arrange　　　　　　　　　　Front

| 35 |

Two Section

まだまだ人気のツーセクションスタイルは、トップに柔らかいパーマをオン。アウトラインは刈り上げず、グラデーションで甘さを出すのがポイント。レイヤーを入れることで今っぽいスタイルが完成する。

Creating soft permed and layered top while not shaving the outline too short, this is a playful updated two section style.

model:Go

Front　　　　　　　　　Side　　　　Back　　　Arrange

| 36 |

American Trad

短いスタイルでもゆるくパーマをかけて柔らかい雰囲気を出すことが可能。トップは適度に立体感とフロントの立ち上がりが出るようにするのがポイント。清潔感のある王道の7:3分けスタイルで、トラッドな雰囲気を作ろう。

A short style with softer impression by subtle perm. The cut and styling need to be solidified with hair wax. Parting 7:3 for clean and classic look.

model:Kotaro

Side　　　Back　　　Arrange　　　　　　　Front

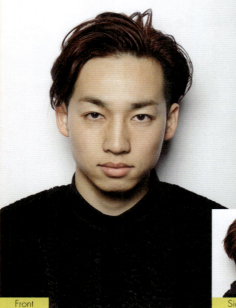

37

Gradation Short

フロントを長めに残した色気のあるスタイル。1度明るくし、そこから深みのあるレッドを入れた綺麗な髪色が雰囲気のある印象を与える。斜め後方にビシッとオールバックにすると、男らしいスタイルに様変わり。

A sexy style with longer front section. Bleached once and colored in beep red for this delicate expression. This can be transformed to a masculine look when the hair is pulled side-back.

model:K.A.I

Side

Back

Arrange

Front

38

Step Layer

パート上にトリマーでラインを入れることで、7:3分けを強調。フォーマルな印象になりがちだが、トップスにスウェットなどを合わせると抜きすぎず、程よいカジュアル感が出せる。スタイリングは、ポマードのツヤ感が必須。

An emphasized 7:3 style by trimming the part line. Style with glossy pomade.

model:Khyohei

Side

Back

Focus

Front

39

Moving Short

逆巻きのパーマをミックスして作り上げた無造作ヘア。ツーブロックにすることで、キリッとした印象もプラス。そんな余裕のある大人なカジュアルスタイルには、ムースやオイルワックスを使って色気を出すのがオススメ。

A tow-blocked mix perm style. Hair mousse or oil wax will add a touch of sensuality to this casual hair.

model:Ryota

Front

Side

Back

Focus

40

Curly Short Layer

ワイルドな印象の彼には、ハーフカールで躍動感をプラス。動きが出るようにフロントとアウトラインは短くしているのがポイントだ。通常は動きを出すが、ボリュームを抑えたスタイルにもアレンジが可能。

A half-curl style with clean front and sides. This can styled both playfully or quiet impression.

model:Yuya

Side

Back

Arrange

Front

41

70's Wave Hair

'70年代のヒッピースタイルをイメージ。今っぽさを出すならワンレングスではなく、顔まわりは軽くするのが肝。半乾きの状態でウェットジュレを揉み込み、自然乾燥で仕上げることができる手軽るさも◎。

The tip for this hippie inspired hair is to give a slight layers along the face line for modern look. Style with wet gel onto half dried hair.

model:Satoru

Front

Side

Back

Arrange

42

Half Curl Gradation

サイドから流れを作った清潔感のあるスタイル。表面にゆるいパーマで動きを出すと大人っぽく仕上がる。さらに、7:3の分け目にラインを入れることで、アレンジでエッジの効いた印象が作れる。

A clean style with smooth length transition from the sides to the back. Adding soft perm will create mature look to the style.

model:Yuki

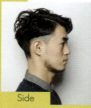
Side

Back

Arrange

Front

43

Mods Short

顔立ちのはっきりした彼は、バングを厚めにして知的な印象に。額を出すスタイリングに飽きてきた人には、ぜひ挑戦してもらいたいヘアスタイルだ。スタイリングは少量のグリースをなじませ、コームでとかすだけでOK。

A sophisticated look with heavy bangs. All you need to do is apply grease lightly and comb.

model:Masanobu

Front

Side

Back

Arrange

44

Square Very Short

柔らかい空気感の彼は、サイドをしっかりと刈り上げてエッジーさを演出。さらに、アッシュゴールドの髪色が個性をプラス。アレンジではグリースをつけ、コームでフロントをなでつければモードな印象に変化する。

Tightly shaved sides for an edgy style. Colored in ash-gold. This style can also look smart when it's greased and combed.

model:Tatsuaki

Side

Back

Arrange

Front

45

Side Gradation

フロントとトップを長めにした、映画『ターミネーター』に出てくる少年、ジョン・コナーのようなヘアスタイル。スタイリングは、グリースを軽くなじませるだけ。オフの日などは、フロントを下ろせば柔らかな印象へと変わる。

This longer top/front style is inspired by John Connor from The Terminator. Easily styled with light grease.

model:Kentaro

Front

Side

Back

Arrange

46

Pompador Style

デヴィット・ボウイの『Heroes』のアルバムジャケットでのヘアスタイルをイメージ。音を感じさせるヘアはモードなTシャツもよく似合う。スタイリングは、ドライヤーを当てながらねじり、マットなワックスで仕上げる。

Referencing the album "Heroes" of David Bowie. For the styling, twist the top with a brush and a dryer then apply matt texture wax for finish.

model:Taisuke

Side

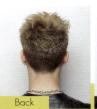
Back

Arrange

Front

47

Square Curly Short

サイドの刈り上げとトップのシルエットをスクエアにして男らしさを演出。パーマをかけた大人なスタイルは、焼けた肌と白いTシャツに相性抜群。アレンジでは、フロントをねじってから出して、ポンパドール風も◎。

A squared silhouette for a masculine look. This curled style can also arranged as a pompadour style.

model:Kei

Front

Side

Back

Arrange

48

Soft Wave Short

ダイアモンドシルエットの緩めのパーマスタイル。全体のフォルムをひし形になるようにカットしアウトラインは短めに。逆巻きと内巻きのパーマをミックスすることでアンニュイな雰囲気のヘアスタイルが完成する。

A soft perm style with diamond silhouette cut. The random perm will create natural impression.

model:Ryotaro

Side

Back

Arrange

Front

49

Reverse Curl

全体的に動きが出るように、リバースパーマをかけたショートスタイル。ハチ部分を逆巻にすることで、骨格補正しつつ毛先の動きを楽しめる。もみあげだけ刈り上げて、メリハリを付ければアクティヴな印象に。

An active gradation cut with reversed perm. Shaving the sideburns will give a youthful impression.

model:Yoshiki

Front

Side

Back

Arrenge

50

Very Short Wolf

伸びかけボウズは、アウトラインを少し長めにして縦長フォルムに。ヤンキー風にならないように、適度な残し方と柔らかな質感にすることがポイント。ハイトーンのベージュ系にして柔らかさを出すと、雰囲気がアップする。

Creating a vertical silhouette with light beige color for those trying to grow their hair from shaved head.

model:Jun

Side

Back

Arrenge

Front

51

Short Layer

ハチ下のグラデーションとトップのレイヤーのバランスが重要なショートスタイル。サイドは低めの刈り上げにし、バックは指で持てる程度に設定。清潔感がありつつ動きもある好感度抜群のヘアスタイルが完成。

A carefully balanced short cut. The layered top and shorter rear transition is the key for this cut. Creating clean and active impression.

model:Kazuki

Side

Back

Arrenge

Front

52

Side Gradation Short

'80年代に流行したサイドグラデーションスタイル。フロントサイドからバックサイドに流れるように作るスタイルは、シンプルながらも品のある美しいシルエットに。フロントを上げればアクティブなヘアスタイルに。

A simple side gradation cut style from 80's. This classy flow can be arranged by pulling the front up for active style.

model:Tatsunori

Side

Back

Arrenge

Front

53

Side Gradation × Perm

毛先がハネやすいように、ハチ上にレイヤーを入れて動きを出す。パーマをかけることで、柔らかな雰囲気とアクティヴな印象を合わせ持つスタイルに。スタイリングはハンドブローの後にウェット感のあるオイルワックスをオン。

An active layered style with perm, finished with glossy oil wax.

model:Naoto

Side

Back

Focus

54

Twist Spiral

'70年代の伝説的なスケートチーム Z-BOYS の中心メンバー、トニー・アルバからインスパイア。コイルの様なパーマがポイントだ。ヘアスタイルにインパクトがるので、洋服はシンプルな無地Tシャツでも充分。

Inspired by a legendary skateboarder Tony Alva. Hard permed style can be bundled for different look.

model:Raymond

Front

Side

Back

Arrange

Short Mohawk

定番スタイルのショートモヒカン。トップに長さを残し、頭の形に合わせてシザーで刈り上げて立体的に仕上げる。スポーティ、清潔感、男らしさを兼ね備えたスタイルは、幅広いシーンにマッチする。

An allrounder style for sporty, clean, masculine look for any occasion. Cut carefully for solidified and balanced silhouette.

model:Makibi

Front

Side

Back

Arrange

GONZ Short

ヘアタイトル通り、レジェンドスケーターのマーク・ゴンザレスをイメージしたパーマスタイル。あえて野暮ったい雰囲気を出すのがポイント。全体を丸いフォルムにし、ソフトな質感のパーマとオイルワックスで仕上げる。

A permed style to recreate a renowned skateboarder Mark Gonzales's hair. Heavy, round silhouette is finished with oil wax.

model:Daisuke

Side

Back

Arrange

Front

57

Curly Short

アメリカを代表するロックミュージシャンの1人、ボブ・ディランをイメージ。重めの縦長フォルムのベースカットにメリハリのあるリッジパーマをかける。強いくせっ毛のような自然な立体感が生まれるのが特徴だ。

Reminding the style of Bob Dylan, this style is made by vertical form with ridge perm,

model:Yusuke

Side

Back

Arrenge

Front

58

Wavy Bob

前上がりのワンレングススタイル。頭のハチから下にウェーブをプラスすることで、硬い髪でも直毛でも柔らかさを出すことが可能。アレンジで、両サイドを耳にかけて額を出すことで、男っぽいスタイルが完成する。

A wavy uni-length for softer impression. Tucking the side hair behind ears for manly impression.

model:Keisuke

Side

Back

Arrenge

Front

Asymmetry Short

片サイドをモヒカンラインまで刈り込んだツーブロック。トップに残した髪に柔らかさを出すことでハードさとソフトさを兼ね備えたスタイルが完成する。スタイリングはシアバターを毛先にラフに馴染ませるだけでOK。

Sectioned in two block; creating soft texture on top will give brisk feel to the look. Style lightly with sheer butter.

model:Takurou

Front

Side

Back

Arrenge

60

Punky Short

パンクやメロコアなどの音楽性が感じられるヘアスタイル。ランダムにカットしつつ、フォルムをしっかりとキープ。カラーリングでしっかりとハイブリーチし、薄いペールアッシュをプラスするとより雰囲気がアップする。

Created by random cut with balanced silhouette. Adding a pale ash hue will help the stylish impression to this punk music inspired style.

model:Yuki

Side

Back

Arrenge

Front

part 2
GOOD HAIR SNAP IN TOWN

街中で見かけた髪型の優良サンプルをスナップ

原宿や渋谷、青山には、いつの時代も最新のトレンドが溢れている。
ここでは、そんな街中で撮影クルーが見つけたグッドヘアスタイルを
スナップで紹介しよう。

we spotted hairstyle samples on streets.

Harajuku/Shibuya/Aoyama area is always the place to find the latest looks.
Here are the snapshots of some good hairstyles we found in this Tokyo's best trend hunt area.

name	平本 兼一
job	スタイリスト
age	28
My Style is	

01

「流行を意識しない、振り切ったヘアスタイルが好きです。この髪型は気に入っていますが、アレンジが一切効かないのが悩みです……」

"Not into 'trendy' styles. I'd rather go with extreme and I do like my current hair though, only disappointment would be can't arrange this one."

name	藤岡 マリア
job	SHOP STAFF
age	21
My Style is	

02

「Gillian Zinser のヘアスタイルはいつも参考にしています。ラフでもキマるっていうのが理想ですね!」

"I like effortless look and I don't put too much thing on my hair. Gillian Zinser's hair style is cute."

name	IRIKI
job	RADD LOUNGE
age	32
My Style is	

03

「個人的にはウェットな質感が好きで、スタイリング剤にもジェルを使用しています。次はスキンヘッドにしようかな」

"I like wet texture with hair gel, but maybe skinhead wouldn't be too bad for my next choice."

name	薬師 雅人
job	THE CONTEMPORARY FIX プレス
age	34
My Style is	「髪の毛の量が多いので、スタイリング剤にはハードなグリースを使用することが多いです。次は髪を伸ばしたスタイルにするつもり」

04

"I use hard texture grease for my thick and volumed hair. I think I'm gonna grow it out."

name	菅野 楽
job	やいやい STAFF
age	24
My Style is	「クールな印象が好きなので前髪を上げてセットすることが多いです。嫌なことがあってスッキリしたい時は、サロンに行って刈り上げます」

05

"I tend to pull my bangs up for clean look. I'd get my hair shaved when I have a bad day, haha"

name	西尾 紗耶香
job	JEWELLERY SHOP STAFF
age	31
My Style is	「ヘアスタイルは季節の移り変わりに合わせて変えることが多いです。次はおかっぱヘアにしてみようかな」

06

"I may change my hair seasonally. One length bob might be my next choice."

name	辻 慶子
job	SHOW CASE by plumpynuts
age	28
My Style is	「髪が細くてスタイリングが決まりにくいのが悩み。イメチェンをするとしたらベリーショートにチャレンジしたい！」

07

"I sometimes find difficult with my extremely fine/thin hair. If I'd have a makeover, I'd try very-short hairstyle."

name	須賀 真之介
job	PEEK-A-BOO STAFF
age	27
My Style is	「あまり作り込み過ぎない自然なウェーブ感を意識しています。ジョニー・デップはいつの時代も自分のスタイルがあってカッコイイと思いますね」

08

"I'm trying to bring just right amount of waves for natural feel to my style. Johnny Depp is my all-time favorite for someone with own style."

name	佐藤 久美子
job	COMME des GARÇON SHOP STAFF
age	34
My Style is	「重さのある髪型が好きで、セットはだいたい10分ぐらいで終わります。コレクションのヴィジュアルはいつも参考にしてますね」

09

"I like hairstyle with some weight/density. it takes me 10 minutes to set my hair everyday. My reference is collection visuals from fashion brands."

name	安藤 友典
job	COMME des GARÇON SHOP STAFF
age	31
My Style is	「自分のヘアスタイルは10年近く変えてません。髪型の参考にしているのは漫画『バガボンド』の主人公、宮本武蔵ですね（笑）」

10

"I haven't changed my hairstyle for a decade. My hairstyle reference? Musashi Miyamoto from a comic book 'Vagagbond.'lol "

name	Johnny
job	John's by Johnny DESIGNER
age	30
My Style is	「自分のこだわりは"派手"さ。このヘアスタイルはグリースを使ってセットしています。髪型の参考は……、昔の人ですかね(笑)」

11

"How I keep my hair? 'flashy.' I use grease for this one. My hairstyle reference…people in the…past, I guess."

name	大湊 由美
job	WTW SURF CLUB STAFF
age	28
My Style is	「髪のボリュームが出ないのが悩み。ヘアスタイルを変えるとしたら、大屋カナさんみたいなロングヘアにしてみたいです！」

12

"I wanna have much volume on my hair. If I'm changing my style, I'd wanna try long hair style like my favorite model."

name	江崎 聡
job	FASHION STYLIST
age	32
My Style is	「サイドを刈上げたスタイルが最近は好き。髪型の参考にしているのはCHALLENGERというブランドの田口さんです」

13

"I like shaved sides styles. My style reference is Mr. Taguchi from fashion imprint CHALLENGER."

name	MARIA VICTORIA
job	PIZZA SLICE STAFF
age	20
My Style is	「毎日のセットにかける時間は2分ぐらい、自然な感じが好きです。モデルのFaith Picozziのヘアスタイルはいつも参考になる！」

14

"it takes 2 minutes to set my hair everyday. I like natural look. Faith Picozzi7s hair style is always inspiring!"

name	K.A.I
job	RADD LOUNGE STAFF
age	22
My Style is	「スタイリング剤にはCOOL GREASEというメーカーのグリースを使ってタイトな髪型になるようにセットしています」

15

"I like this COOL GREASE brand for neat and tidy styling."

name	春田 栞
job	PEEK-A-BOO STAFF
age	24
My Style is	「ベリーショートだけど、女性らしいポイントを残したスタイルです。次はストレートなロングヘアにしようか悩み中」

16

"I keep feminine touch to my very short style. Thinking about long straight hair for my next style..."

name	Giani Hirako
job	Sota
age	21
My Style is	「キメ過ぎは好きじゃないから、いつも自然な感じ。映画『Lords of Dogtown』にでてくるジェイのスタイルがカッコイイね」

17

"Too-much-polished style is not really my thing so I'd just keep it like this. Have you seen Jay from "Lords of Dogtown?" He's pretty cool."

name	盛川 雄祐
job	Caliente DEPUTY MANAGER
age	26

My Style is

18

「自然体なヘアスタイルが好きで、よく海外のバンドマンたちの髪型を参考にしています。次はモヒカンにしてみたい！」

"I like natural styles and music band crews are my hairstyle reference. I wanna try mohawk!"

name	Rena
job	Flying Tiger Copenhagen SHOP STAFF
age	27

My Style is

19

「髪のカラーリングにはいつもこだわっていますね、次にイメージチェンジするとしたら、ロングヘアにトライしてみたい」

"I carefully choose my hair color every time I change it. I'd try long hair style next."

name	川手 恭治
job	DANCER
age	24

My Style is

20

「基本的にはサッパリ＆スッキリの短髪が好きです。スタイリングも30秒ぐらいで済ませますね（笑）。いつかアフロとかもやってみたいな」

"I like to keep it simple and clean. I only spare 30 seconds for my hair every morning, lol. Flo would be dope tho."

name	岩瀬 大祐
job	PEEK-A-BOO STAFF
age	29
My Style is	「バキっと決め過ぎないように、ジェルでラフにかきあげてセットしています。次はベリーショートか縛れる位の長さにしたい」

21

"My current mood is to play with the bottom part. Rita Ora is my style reference."

name	根本 愛莉
job	Montoak スタッフ
age	26
My Style is	「ねこっ毛なので、子供っぽくならないようにセットしています。お洒落なショップのスタッフさんをよく参考にしていますね」

22

"I'm trying not to look childish. My references are stylish people at stores."

name	酒井 まい
job	Vithmic Model Agency
age	22
My Style is	「ヘアスタイルはナチュラルなイメージでいつもセットしてます。Schwarzkoph のエアーワックスが使いやすくてお気に入り」

23

"I like natural finish on my hair. My favorite styling product is the air-wax from Schwarzkoph."

name	山本 航
job	San Francisco Peaks STAFF
age	25
My Style is	「特にこだわりがあるわけじゃないけど男らしい髪型は好き。次にヘアスタイルを変えるとしたらモヒカンにしてみようかな」

24

"I don't have too much 'thing' for my hair though, I like masculine styles. I might wanna try a mohawk style next."

name	セーリィー クリスティーナ 美怜
job	American Apparel STAFF
age	21
My Style is	「季節の変わり目にヘアスタイルを変えることが多いです。次に変えるならベリーショートかグルグルパーマにしたい！」

"I tend to change my hairstyles in between seasons. My next choice is either very-short or hard permed style."

name	垂口 友輝
job	Carbon STAFF
age	28
My Style is	「普段からオールバックスタイルが基本です。ヘアスタイルを参考にしているのは野村訓市さん、黒ぶち眼鏡も買っちゃおうかな……」

26

"Combed back hair is my default style. My reference is Mr. Kunichi Nomura. Should I get glasses like him too…?"

name	大滝 幾巳
job	cafe STAFF
age	24
My Style is	「とにかく"楽に早く"セットできる、というのが自分のヘアスタイルのモットーです。髪型を変えたくなるのはスッキリした時！」

27

"My hairstyle motto is 'fast and easy.' I feel like changing my hair when I get refreshed."

name	浦島 愛可
job	PEEK-A-BOO STAFF
age	22
My Style is	「左側をいつも耳にかけてスッキリさせるのがこだわり。最近は前髪がずっと長めなので、眉毛に乗るくらい短くしてみたいです！」

28

"I always tuck my hair behind the ear on left side. I am thinking about shorten my bangs to my eyebrows."

name	SAAYA COATES KANAI
job	PIZZA SLICE STAFF
age	22
My Style is	「ラフなのに、キマるヘアスタイルが好きです。いつかピーターパンに出てくるタイガー・リリーの髪型にしたい！」

29

"I like naturally styled hair. I'd wanna do Tiger Lily from Peter-Pan's hair someday!"

name	岩村 綾乃
job	APPAREL STAFF
age	26
My Style is	「ポマードなどでウェットな質感を出すのが自分なりのコダワリ。洋服の系統が変わる時にヘアスタイルも変えることが多いかな」

30

"I like wet look with pomade. I tend to change my hairstyles when I go for different fashion styles."

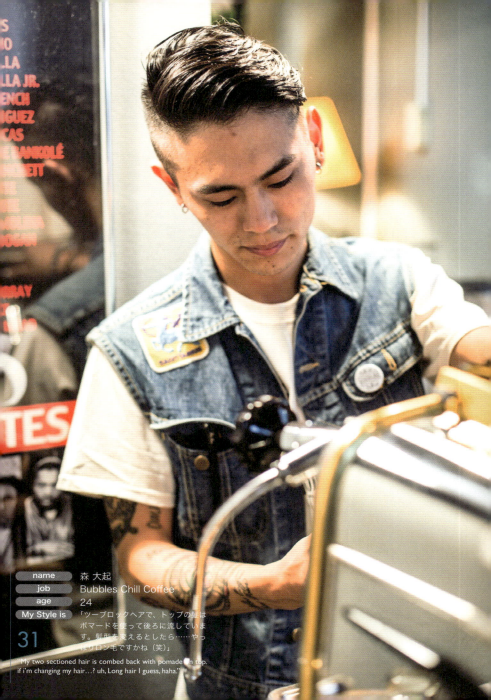

name	森 大起
job	Bubbles Chill Coffee
age	24
My Style is	「ツーブロックヘアで、トップの髪はポマードを使って後ろに流しています。髪型を変えるとしたら……やっぱりロン毛ですかね（笑）」

"My two sectioned hair is combed back with pomade on top. if i'm changing my hair…? uh, Long hair I guess, haha."

name	ウッディ
job	San Francisco Peaks STAFF
age	24

32

My Style is 「ロングヘアはセットいらずだし意外に楽チンなんです。唯一の悩みは、髪を乾かすのが面倒くさいことぐらいですね（笑）」

"Long hair style is pretty easy to set. it only takes time to dry. haha"

name	aoi
job	FREE GALLERY SHOP STAFF
age	21

33

My Style is 「ブラック〜アッシュのグラデーションカラーが自分でも気に入っています。髪型はいつも飽きたら無意識に変えてるかな」

"I like this gradation coloring now. I change my hair randomly whenever I feel like to change it."

name	岩瀬 千香
job	PEEK-A-BOO STAFF
age	25

34

My Style is 「襟足に変化を出したヘアスタイルが最近の気分。参考にしてる有名人はリタ・オラ、気分を変えたい時に髪型も変えることが多いです」

"I hand-comb with gel for rough look. I want either make it very short or grow it long enough to tie it."

name	YOKO
job	LOCALS ONLY STAFF
age	26

35

My Style is 「少しウェット感を出したイメージが最近は好きです。次に髪型を変えるとしたらスーパーロングヘアにトライしたい！」

"I'm into slightly wet look lately. I'd wanna try super long hair style."

name	YAH-MAN
job	THE GREAT BURGER MANAGER
age	29

My Style is

36

「ラフな感じが好きで、セットも少しウェットになるオイルワックスで後ろに流すくらい。次は金髪にでもしてみようかな」

"I normally keep rough-style hair with oil wax. I may wanna dye my hair blonde next time."

name	成田 有彩
job	PEEK-A-BOO STAFF
age	22

My Style is

37

「自分の中でユニセックス感が今の気分です。セットはジェルワックスを使って少しラフなイメージで仕上げるようにしています」

"Unisex look is my current mood. I use gel-wax to my hair styling with natural image."

name	高橋 健人
job	Restaurant Casita MANAGER
age	34

My Style is

38

「仕事が飲食業なので、ヘアスタイルは清潔感を第一にしています。普段からジェルを使って後ろにかき上げたスタイルが定番ですね」

"Since I work in food industry, cleanliness is the priority. I default style is combed back style with hair gel."

name	竹田あき
job	APPAREL STAFF
age	20

My Style is

39

「最近はこの重めためワンレングスにハマっています。髪の毛が乾燥しやすいので少しウェットな感じにするのもこだわりの1つ!」

"I like this current one length style now. My hair gets dried easily so I'd style with a bit wetted look."

name	芝本 智美
job	the 3rd Burger 青山骨董通り店 STAFF
age	27

My Style is

40

「ここ最近は、ちょっと赤みがかったボブをずっとキープしています。次は前髪をめっちゃ短くしようか悩み中……」

"I've been keeping my reddish burnet bob style for a while. Thinking about having much shorter bangs."

name	富田 俊太郎
job	Carhartt WIP STAFF
age	19
My Style is	「あまり時間がかからずに、すぐキマりやすいスタイルが気に入っています。髪型の参考にしているの長瀬智也さんです！」

41

"This doesn't take much time to style and I like that. Mr. Tomoya Nagase is my style reference!"

name	長谷川 夏子
job	PEEK-A-BOO STAFF
age	25
My Style is	「ヘアスタイルは何か気持ちに変化が欲しい時に変えますね。と言っても、最近はずっとショートなので、いつかロングにしたい！（笑）」

42

"I've been keeping my hair short for a while. I do wanna to try long hair someday!"

name	佐々木 由美
job	PEEK-A-BOO STAFF
age	24
My Style is	「コンパクトなシルエットのボブスタイルが最近のお気に入り。担当スタイリストさんに相談しながら髪型を変えることが多いです」

43

"I like minimal clean silhouette bob style. I always talk to my hairstylist when I try different styles"

name	Yusuke
job	DESIGNER
age	30
My Style is	

44

「ポマードを使って、いつも横に撫で付けるようにセットしてます。鳥肌実のスタイルが好きで、髪型も参考にしていますね」

"I use pomade and comb my hair to the side. I like Minoru Tohihada style."

name	DEAD KEBAB
job	MUSICIAN
age	--
My Style is	

45

「ナチュラルな印象が好きなので、普段からスタイリングには時間をかけません。髪型を変えるのはライヴの時ぐらいですね」

"I won't put too much product on my hair. I change or arrange my hairstyle only when I go on stage for my performance."

name	増田 有里
job	PEEK-A-BOO STAFF
age	21
My Style is	「あえて動きを出さないストレートで、大人っぽく＆格好良い印象にセットしています。時間もあまりかけず5分ぐらいで完成しますね」

46

"Mature and sophisticated straight look is what I'm looking for for my hair. I only spend 5 minutes to set my hair"

name	関口 敦士
job	Attractions STAFF
age	30
My Style is	「髪の量が多いのでポマードなどを使ってセットしています。トップは手ぐしでラフに、サイドはコームで流すのがコダワリです」

47

"I use pomade to set my hair with comb for the sides an hands for my top section."

name	涌田 文香
job	M.Y.O.B NYC STAFF
age	26
My Style is	「ただ普通なヘアスタイルは嫌なので、どこかしらに色を入れたりするのが好きですね。いつかブレイズとかもやってみたいな」

48

"Making it different is my style. Just like having a colored part on my hair etc… I wanna get braided someday"

name	吉見 彩
job	PEEK-A-BOO STAFF
age	28
My Style is	「自然な動きとツヤを出すのがスタイルのこだわっているポイント。気分と季節によってヘアスタイルも変えるのが好きですね」

49

"What i try to keep to my hairstyle are natural glow and flow I like changing my hair seasonally or go for it with my mood."

name	酒井 元太
job	Damage done SHOP STAFF
age	27
My Style is 50	「サイドを刈り上げるのが自分なりのヘアスタイルのこだわりです。次に挑戦するとしたら、このまま伸ばして長髪にしてみたいな」

"Shaved sides is sorta my thing. I may wanna grow my hair out till it gets much much longer."

Part
3
STYLIST'S LIFE STYLE

TOKYO HAIRを創出する
ヘアスタイリストに密着

TOKYO HAIRを創り上げる、ヘアスタイリスト5名にフォーカス。
そのクリエイティビティの源を探るべく密着取材を敢行。
それぞれの個性際立つライフスタイルは一見の価値あり！

Close coverage to Tokyo's hairstylist.

Getting up-close to five hairstylist who create "TOKYO HAIR."
Their unveiled unique lifestyles are worth to see!

PEEK-A-BOO 青山店トップスタイリスト

佐藤 学
Manabu Sato

髪型を一任されるのが、最高に嬉しくて楽しい

「僕が美容師を志したころ、世間では美容師ブームの真っ只中でした。原宿界隈にたくさんの美容室ができる中、PEEK-A-BOOは確固たるスタイルを貫いていて、それがすごくカッコよかったんです。入社してからは、毎日が楽しいことの連続で辛いと思ったことは本当に1度もないんですよ。自分を指名してくれて、他愛もない会話をして、自分の好きなスタイルが作れるなんて最高じゃないですか!「お任せします」と言われると、本当に嬉しいですね。PEEK-A-BOOには個性的な先輩がたくさんいるので、まずは追いつき、そして超えられるように頑張ります」。

Customers are counting on me.
That's what I get excited and thankful for.

"It was such a popular occupation to be a hairstylist when I was also wanted to be one. There were so many hair salons in Harajuku but PEEK-A-BOO stood out to me the most. It's been carrying on their style and has known what they stand for, so I just fell for that. I've seriously enjoyed working here since the day one. It is such an amazing job that people come to me and talk to me while I can create what I believe cool. I get excited every time my customers completely count on me for their hairstyles. PEEK-A-BOO has numbers of talented senior colleagues. I'd always try to learn from them and would love to surpass them someday."

Recommend Shop_01
アートレスエレガントストア「BIN」
Art less elegant store「BIN」

セレクトアイテムがダサめでカッコイイ！

「僕のお客さんでもあり長年の友人でもある.efiLevolのディレクター・阿久津くんがやっているアートレスエレガントストアです。ダサめでカッコイイものが揃っているのはもちろん、阿久津くんの人柄に惹かれて通っています」。

Their stuff is so bad and that's great.

"The store is run by ".efiLevol" director Akutsu. He is my customer and my friend for long time. It is so great that he gather these stupid cool stuff. I always come here for his merchandise selection and his character."

SHOP DATA
東京都目黒区青葉台1-9-6
03・6416・0972
営業時間：12:00～20:00
定休日：無休
URL：shop-tokyo.jp

Recommend Shop_02
オーガニックレストラン「jicca」
Organic restaurant「jicca」

毎週のように通う1番好きな飲食店

「とにかくご飯とワインが美味い！中でも"ギュベジ"というトルコの煮込み料理は絶品なので、ぜひ食べてみてください。仕事終わりにフラリと行ったり、ランチを食べに行ったり。1番よく行く飲食店は間違いなくココです」。

My favorite restaurant. I probably visit every week.

"They serve good wine and good food. This Turkish stew dish called "Güveç" is the one I want you to try. I come here for both lunch break and after work. This is definitely my default spot."

SHOP DATA
東京都渋谷区西原2-27-4
升本ビル2F 奥
03・5738・2235
営業時間：18:00～22:00（月）、
12:00～14:00（火～土）
定休日：日曜
URL：fromjicca.com

Favorite_01
ヒップホップ
Hip Hop Music

30年以上聴き続けてもはや生活の一部

「中学生の頃、MTV で初めてヒップホップの PV を観て以来、ずっと聴き続けています。ハタチの頃は DJ もやっていて、レコードは 500 枚以上持っていたけれど、最近はもっぱら聴く専門。最近は The Internet をよく聴いています」。

I've been listening over 30 years. This is part of my life now.

"I first saw a Hip-Hop music video on MTV when I was in junior high and I've been listening ever since. I used to DJ at the age of 20 or so, so I had over 500 of vinyls. Now I just play in my headphones but the music is a part of me. "The Internet" might be the top of my playlist lately."

FAVORITE DISC

1 『CHAMPION SOUND』 JAYLIB

2 『BLACK ON BOTH SIDES』 MOSDEF

3 『illmatic』 nas

4 『BEATS<RHYMES AND LI』 A TRIBE CALLED QUEST

BEASTIE BOYS TEE !

Favorite_02
自転車
Bicycle

毎日乗るものだから乗りやすさを重視

「通勤で毎日乗っているトレックバイクです。毎日乗るものだから、がっしりとした転びづらそうなものを選びました。池袋の「Y's Road」はサンタクルズのマウンテンバイクなど、面白い自転車が揃っています」。

Functions comes first for my everyday ride.

"I ride this trek bike everyday to work. I chose a durable type so I won't fall over easily. 「Y's Road」 in Ikebukuro carries good selections of mountain bikes like Santa Cruz etc."

Favorite_03
ヘアスタイリング剤
Hair styling products

使用感もコストパフォーマンスも最高

「ワックスは 18 年、ジェルは 10 年くらい愛用しています。過去には金髪から始まって、赤やピンクなど、いろんな色に染めていましたが、ヘアスタイリング剤はずっとこの 2 つ。どちらも PEEK-A-BOO で取り扱っています」。

Best texture with great price-performance.

"I use this hair wax for 18 years, and the gel for a decade. I had all kinds of hair color from blonde, red, or even pink for once. For all those time, I've been using these two for my styling. Both could be found in PEEK-A-BOO."

PEEK-A-BOO ANNEX店トップスタイリスト

神保 樹敏
Shigetoshi Jimbo

周りの人たちの後押しが今の自分を作り上げた

「僕が今、PEEK-A-BOOの美容師として働けているのは、周りの人たちの後押しがあったからと言っても過言ではありません。美容の道に進んだのも、PEEK-A-BOOに興味を持ったのも、友人からのアドバイスがきっかけでした。実際、人と接することやモノを作ることは昔から好きだったので、美容師は天職だと実感してます。1番の喜びは、僕を指名してくれたお客様が笑顔で帰り、次に来たときに「前回も良かった」と言ってくれること。だからこそ、常に成長を続けなければと思っています。スタッフ全員でレベルアップして、良い店を作っていきたいですね」。

I became who I am with the support from people around me.

"I wouldn't be here working as a top stylist in PPEK-A-BOO without tremendous support from my people. My friends taught me about the industry and PEEK-A-BOO. Actually, working with my hands and talking to people has been my forte so this is a perfect job for me. I feel delighted when people come to me and leave with smiles, then come back to me again. To keep my customers happy, I do want to learn more and would like to grow together with my colleagues as a team at this salon."

Favorite_01
家
Home

妻と猫と3人で過ごす時間が最高に幸せ

「休日は家で過ごすことが多いですね。今は妻と猫との3人暮らしですが、来年には家族がもう1人増える予定です。1Fの倉庫でD.I.Y.やバイクをいじったりしていると、あっという間に時間が過ぎていくんですよ」。

**My wife, cat, and me.
The happiest time of my life.**

"I mostly spend my days off at home. My wife and I have a cat so it's three of us now but we are expecting a baby soon. Time just flies when I am working on my D.I.Y. projects and motorcycle in my garage at home."

バイク
「ホンダのXR250のタイヤをオンロードに替えたものと、スズキのバンディット1200を気分によって乗り分けています」。

猫
「ある日、ベランダを見たらベランダに産まれて間もない猫がいて、飼うことになったんです。生命力と運の強さを感じますよね（笑）」。

My name is Mie!

D.I.Y.
「美容師になっていなかったら大工になっていたと思うくらい、物作りが好きなんです。猫のために猫タワーも自作しました」。

Favorite_02
ゴルフ
Golf

年齢を超えた交流や自分との戦いができる

「月に2回ほどラウンドに出ています。年の差に関係なくプレーや交流ができるところや、人との勝負以上に自分自身と勝負するところが好きです。PEEK-A-BOOのスタッフとプレーすることもありますよ。いい結果が出せるように日々の練習や体力作りも欠かせません」。

It's a place for challenging myself and communicating with other generations.

"I play on the round twice a month. What I like about golfing is it is played by various ages and it also bonds us. You will compete with others but also to yourself. I play with PEEK-A-BOO coworkers sometimes too. My workout is for my better score."

Favorite_03
コーヒー
Coffee

豆を煎るところから自分でやるのが楽しい

「美味しいコーヒーが飲みたいと思い、豆を買って飲む分だけ焙煎しています。1Fの倉庫のシャッターを開けてテーブルを出し、コンロと道具一式を持ってきて外で楽しむのが僕の休日の定番の過ごし方です」。

I enjoy roasdting my own cup of coffee.

"I started roasting my own coffee. I get beans and use my roasting equips in my garage. Setting up a table and enjoying my cup is how I spend my day off at home."

PEEK-A-BOO オリンピア店シニアスタイリスト

水舟 勝己
Katsumi Mizufune

直線的なカットにパーマを取り入れたスタイルが得意

「美容師になりたいと最初に思ったのは13歳の時。昔からヘアアレンジが好きだったんです。岡山の専門学校に進み、そのまま地元で働こうと思っていたのですが、PEEK-A-BOOのショーを観て、絶対にここで働きたいと思ったんです。髪を切る姿が本当に芸術的で、あんな風に自分もカットがしたい、と。その思いがあるので、今でもカットを褒められるのが1番嬉しいですね。それから僕はパーマが得意なので、ちょっと人と違うパリッとしたスタイルを提案していけたらと思っています。そして女性だけでなく男性からも支持されるスタイリストになりたいです」。

Straight cut with permed arrange is my forte.

"When I was 13, I knew I wanted to be a hairstylist. I just liked doing hair-arranging since I don't know when. I finished beauty school in Okayama and was going to work at a local salon. That was my plan until I saw PEEK-A-BOO's show. I was so moved and impressed by their artistic cutting technique and wanted to do just like them. That was why I'm here today and I still remember my clear ambition for the cutting skill, so getting compliments about my cut is the best thing for me. I also like doing perm. I'd like to create crisp clean styles for both men and women."

Favorite_01
Rock
Rock Music

ロックやパンクから
パワーをもらっている

「中学生の頃からロックやメロディックパンク、スカなどにハマっていき、今でも毎日のように聴いています。高校の頃にはバンドでドラムを叩いていました。今でも休日に1人でスタジオに入ってドラムを叩いたりしています」。

Rock and Punk is my power source.
"I've been into rock, melodic punk, and ska music since I was in junior high. I started playing drums in a band in high school. I still go to a studio by myself to play on my days off now."

| 1 | 2 |
| 3 | 4 |

FAVORITE DISC

1 『HECTIC E.P.』
OPERATION IVY

2 『ROCK'N'ROLL』
SpecialThanks x MIX MARKET

3 『the dresscords』
the dresscords

4 『FLAVOR FLAVOR』
KEYTALK

Go to Music Live!

ドラムスティック
ケースに入れて持ち歩いている愛用のドラムスティック。地元・岡山で活動していた時には、ハワイアン6などのツアーサポートの経験もあるそうだ。

Favorite_02
メガネ
Eyewear

**毎日掛けるものだから
デザイン重視で選ぶ**

「毎日掛けるものだからこそ、デザインにもこだわって選んでいます。特にお気に入りはOLIVER PEOPLESのメタルのメガネ。さり気ない刻印など、細かなデザインが好きなんです。年に1本のペースで新調しています」。

Design comes first for my everyday eyewear.

"I first saw a Hip-Hop music video on MTV when I was in junior high and I've been listening ever since. I used to DJ at the age of 20 or so, so I had over 500 of vinyls. Now I just play in my headphones but the music is a part of me. "The Internet" might be the top of my playlist lately."

FAVORITE EYEWEAR

1 NO BRAND
2 EFFECTOR
3 OLIVER PEOPLES
4 OLIVER PEOPLES
5 Ray-Ban

Favorite_03
写真
Photography

**何気ない日常の風景を
写真に収めていく**

「約3年前、家族写真を撮ろうと思って一眼レフカメラを購入したのがきっかけで撮るようになりました。娘と一緒に出掛ける時は必ず持ち歩いています。何気ない表情や一緒に出掛けた場所を撮るのが楽しいんですよね」。

Capturing my daily moments on my SLR.

"I bought my SLR 3 years ago when I wanted to take my family portrait. I carry my camera ever since when I take my daughter out. It is just so much fun to take pictures of everyday scenes and places with her."

PEEK-A-BOO 原宿シニアスタイリスト・副店長

西尾 卓義
Takuyoshi Nishio

自分にしかできないデザインを作るのが目標

「専門学生の頃に観たPEEK-A-BOOのヘアショーでの衝撃は今でも忘れられません。川島先生の作るスタイルがあまりにカッコよくて、絶対にPEEK-A-BOOへ入ろうと決意したんです。最近ではサロンワークだけでなく、PEEK-A-BOOのアカデミーで講師も務めているのですが、教えているようで実は自分が学ぶことが多く、常に刺激を受けています。もちろん今でも川島先生や(原宿店の)ボスの伊東からは、あらゆる面で刺激を受け続けています。2人のように、確固たるスタイルを確立し、自分にしかできないものを提供できるようになるのが目標です」。

My goal is to create designs no one else can recreate.

"I can still remember clearly how amazing Mr. Kawashima's styling was at a PEEK-A-BOO hair show. I saw that when I was a student and decided I would work at PEEK-A-BOO no matter what. Now I actually work there and also give lectures at PEEK-A-BOO Academy. I get so much inspirations at both places even if I set myself as a teacher at the academy. My biggest mentors would be both the founder Mr. Kawashima and Ito from our Harajuku store. I'd want to have my very own style and aesthetic to create original hair design, just like those two."

Favorite_01
写真
Photography

サロンのヴィジュアル写真も担当するほどの腕前

「本格的に写真を撮り始めたのはPEEK-A-BOOに入社してからです。自分の作ったヘアスタイルを撮ることからスタートして、今ではPEEK-A-BOOのヴィジュアル写真やムービーはほとんど僕が撮影しています」

As good as being a photographer for salon's visual campaigns.

"The store is run by ".efiLevol" director Akutsu. He is my customer and my friend for long time. It is so great that he gather these stupid cool stuff. I always come here for his merchandise selection and his character."

USE IT!
CANON EOS 5D MarkII

Favorite_02
スケート&ピスト
Skateboarding & Pist bike

休みの日の息抜きに欠かせない相棒

「休みの日は二子玉川や駒沢公園でスケートをすることが多いですね。ピストバイクは自分で組んだものに乗っています。最近では移動するときに乗る程度ですけど、以前はメッセンジャーのレースに出たりもしていました」。

My buddies on my day off.

"I go skateboarding at Komazawa park or Futakotamagawa on holidays. The bike was built on my own. I just ride this as my city commute though, I used to ride on messenger races."

Recommend Shop_01
フラワーショップ「DILIGENCE PARLOUR」
Flower shop「DILIGENCE PARLOUR」

男性にオススメのフラワーショップ

「自宅はもちろん、店舗のグリーンも DILIGENCE PARLOUR（ディリジェンスパーラー）で選んでいます。フローリストの越智くんに相談すれば、必ず素敵な花やグリーンに出会えます。お客さんも男性が多いそうなので、ぜひ行ってみてください！」

The florist I recommend for men.

"I get plants for both my home and salon from "DILIGENCE PARLOUR." The florist Ochi would give you the best advice for flowers and greens. The store has quite a number of male customers so I'd want you to pop by as well."

SHOP DATA
東京都渋谷区神宮前4-26-24 シアタープロダクツ表参道内
03・6438・1757
営業時間：12:00 〜 20:00
定休日：木曜・日曜
URL：diligenceparlour.jp

Favorite_03
SUNSEA の洋服
Clothing brand「SUNSEA」

デザインが好きで着続けているブランド

「SUNSEAの洋服は、シンプルなデザインの中に遊びが入っているのが好きで、ブランド立ち上げ時からずっと着ています。左のパーカはデザイナーの米山さんが僕のために作ってくれた、世界に1つだけしかないスペシャルなものです！」

I keep wearing their design for long time.

"I love how they take simple designs and give a touch of creativity to it. I wear "SUNSEA" since the brand first launched. The designer Mr. Yoneyama designed this parka exclusively for me!"

PEEK-A-BOO 原宿スタイリスト

岩崎 桃子
Momoko Iwasaki

個人の眠っている魅力を
引き出せるのがPEEK-A-BOO

「専門学生のころ、PEEK-A-BOOにはお客さんとして通っていたんです。ずっと伸ばしていたロングヘアをボブにして新しい自分を見つけてもらい、すごく感動しました。その後、原宿店代表の伊東が掲載されている雑誌を読み、こんなにカッコイイ大人がいるんだと驚き、PEEK-A-BOO入社を志しました。まだ若手スタイリストですが、当面の目標はトップスタイリストになることです。私の直属の上司が、女性で初めてトップスタイリストになった人だったので、絶対に追いつきたいです!」。

PEEK-A-BOO awakens one's hidden charm.

"I used to come to PEEK-A-BOO as a customer when I was a student. Back then, they gave me an amazing makeover from long hair to bob style and I felt so happy for it. Later on, I read an article of our current art director Mr. Ito and got impressed by his style. That's how I decided to work at PEEK-A-BOO. It's been only a year since I work as a stylist so my goal for now is to be a top stylist. My direct senior colleague is the first female top stylist in PEEK-A-BOO so I really want to reach her someday."

Favorite_01

海外旅行
Traveling abroad

**旅先での出会いが
日々の刺激になる**

「特別休暇を利用して海外旅行に毎年行っています。イギリス、フランス、イタリア、オーストリア、チェコ………。今年はスペインに行ってきました。イタリアで出会った彫金師の方とは今でも連絡を取り合っているんですよ」。

As good as being a photographer for salon's visual campaigns.

"I always use my vacation time for traveling overseas every year. I've visited England, France, Italy, Australia, Czech, and this year for Spain. I still keep in touch with a chaser in Italy."

Recommend Shop_01

セレクトショップの DELTA
Select shop「DELTA」

感度の高いお洒落アイテムが見つかる

「世界中からセレクトされたオシャレでひとクセあるアイテムが揃うお店です。時期によって雰囲気がガラリと変わるのでワクワクしながら通っています。私はHOPEのパンツがお気に入りで、何度かリピート買いしています」。

Always find well selected items.

" The store carries international brands' unique items. Their selection and display change drastically every season so I can get excited every time I visit. I've bought my favorite pairs of pants from "HOPE" at this store repeatedly."

SHOP DATA
東京都渋谷区西原 3-4-3
03・3485・0933
営業時間：13:00～21:00（月～金）、
12:00～20:00（土日祝）
定休日：火曜
URL：www.deltaonline.jp

Favorite_02
帽子
Cap & Hat

ボブヘアにしてから必要不可欠な存在

「ボブだとヘアアレンジが限られてしまうので、帽子で変化を楽しんでいます。全部で100個くらい持っているのですが、特にCA4LAのベレー帽は色違いで揃えるくらいお気に入り。最近はキャップもよく被ります!」

These are part of me since I got bob hair.

"Because bob hair wouldn't have much selection of style arrangement, I use headwear for different looks. I may have a hundred of them actually. My favorites would be berets from "CA4LA," and I started wearing more caps lately."

FAVORITE CAP&HAT

1 AntonioGatto
2 Racal
3 CA4LA
4 URBAN RSEARCH

HAND MADE!

Favorite_03
スノードーム
Snow Dome

見た目の可愛さとキラキラ感の虜に

「6年前、フィレンツェのスノードーム専門店で購入したのをきっかけに集め出しました。カナダのトゥインクル社のものは土台が可愛くて、オーストリアのパージー社のものはキラキラが細かくてキレイなんですよ」。

The flossy glitters and adorable shapes totally got me.

"I started collecting snow globes 6 years ago when I visited a store in Florence. Canadian brand Twinkle makes really pretty outerbase and Perzy from Australia has such a fine and beautiful flakes in the dome."

Part
4

TOP RUNNER'S HAIR STYLE

個性際立つ
著名人のヘアスタイル

PEEK-A-BOOの確かな技術と時代を的確に捉えるスタイルは、多くの著名人たちをも魅了する。ここでは性別も年齢も職業も違う5人の著名人のスタイルを紐解いていく。

Hairstyles of Tokyo celebrities.

PEEK-A-BOO plays huge role behind the distinctive hairstyles for variety of people in different fields. These are five public figures in Tokyo who count on PEEK-A-BOO's style creation.

01

谷原 章介
俳優

1972年生まれ。1992年より約2年間、集英社『MEN'S NON-NO』の専属モデルとして活躍。その後、数々の舞台や映画、ドラマなど幅広いフィールドで役者として活躍中。

Born in 1972. Shosuke Tanihara started his carrier as an exclusive model for "MEN'S NON-NO"magazine from SHUEISHA, working for two years from 1992. Now he is working on a variety of plays, movies and TV dramas.

一問一答 Question&Answer

Q PEEK-A-BOO に通ってどれくらいですか？
A 10年とちょっとぐらいです
Q 伊東さんに担当してもらうようになったキッカケは？
A 担当して頂いているヘアメイクさんが PEEK-A-BOO の出身で、その方に紹介して頂きました
Q 何を参考に髪型を決めていますか？
A その時々の演じる役によって担当の伊東さんに相談しながら決めています。伊東さんの名前を作品のエンドロールに入れたいぐらい頼っていますね
Q 1度やってみたい髪型は？
A やっぱりモヒカンですね。キャラクター的に僕はなかなかできないと思うから（笑）

Q How long have you been coming to PEEK-A-BOO?
A For just over 10 years.
Q Why did you choose Mr. Ito to style your hair?
A Another hairstylist from PEEK-A-BOO introduced me to him.
Q What influences you when you choose a new hairstyle?
A I ask Mr Ito for advice. It depends on what role I'm playing at the time. He helps me so much that I should put his name on the credits.
Q What hairstyle do you want to try in your lifetime?
A Mohawk! No doubt about it. But I barely have a chance to try new styles because of my character.

谷原さんの髪型のキーワードは、"さりげなさ"と"自然体"。大人の余裕を感じさせる爽やかさが特徴です。具体的には、サイドからのグラデーションカットでトップのレイヤーは甘め。フロントは若干長めに残して、耳上と毛先にセニングで軽さを出しています。スタイリングも柔らかめのワックスを軽く毛先につけて、自然に流すぐらいが丁度良いと思います。

Hidehiko Ito

担当スタイリスト
伊東 秀彦
PEEK-A-BOO 原宿店 アートディレクター

The keywords, which describe Mr. Tanihara's hairstyle, are "casual" and "natural. His look provides some refinement as a mature man. Both sides are created by a gradation cut and the top layer has a light finish. The front section is left a bit long, around the ears and the tips are thinned to be light. I would recommend using soft textured hair wax to the tips and allow your hair to flow naturally.

02 レイザーラモンHG
お笑い芸人

1975年生まれ。レイザーラモンRGとともにお笑いコンビ、レイザーラモンとして活動。2005年、流行語大賞に「フォーーー！」がノミネートされ大ブレークを果たす。その後、プロレスへの参戦などを経て、2013年にはTHE MANZAIで決勝に進出し、再ブレイク。
instagram.com/razorramonhg

Born in 1975. HG Works with RG as part of a comic duo "Razor Ramon". HG became a smash hit with his catchphrase: "Fooooooo!!" that was also nominated on "Ryuko-go Taisho" (Buzzword award) in 2005. After training as a pro-wresler he gained in popularity that took him to the finals of the TV comedy contest show "The Manzai" in 2013. instagram.com/razorramonhg

一問一答 Question&Answer

Q PEEK-A-BOOに通い始めたきっかけは？
A 奥さんの紹介です

Q 今の髪型にした経緯を教えてください
A 堅くて量が多くてクセもあるので短髪はマストです。子どもが2人いて40歳になったので、爽やかなお父さんに見えるように相談しました

Q 今のヘアスタイルのポイントは？
A とにかく手入れがしやすいのでポイントです（笑）。直毛だからセットする必要がないんですよ。

Q やってみたい髪型は？
A サラサラのロングヘアですね。若いころ伸ばしたら、堅すぎてまったく風になびかず岩ノリみたいになったので……（笑）

Q How did you find out about to PEEK-A-BOO?
A Through my wife.

Q Why did you decide to get your current hairstyle?
A My hair has a lot of volume and it's hard and frizzy, so short hair is essential. I asked to look like a cool dad because I've turned forty and have two children.

Q What hair style point?
A It was hard to find out the best hairstyle for me because my hair is straight and thick. I asked him for a clean-looking style that is easy to maintain.

Q What hairstyle do you want to try in your lifetime?
A Straight long hair. I tried it once when I was younger, mine looked like Rock Laver (a type of seaweed) and it didn't flow at all in the wind...

> すごく男前で俳優さんのようなHGさん。毛量が多くて堅く、髪自体が立ってしまうので、できる髪型が限られてはくるのですが、今のスタイルは髪質的にベストですし、爽やかな雰囲気にもよく似合っていると思います。乾かすだけで今のスタイルになりますが、仕上げにウエット感のあるジェルを馴染ませると、ツヤ感が出るのでオススメです。

He is very good looking and looks like an actor. Only a few hairstyles will suit him because he has a lot of hair, it's thick and it stands up naturally. Now he has the best style considering his hair features and it matches his fresh character. The styling is accomplished by just letting the hair dry naturally but I would recommend putting some wet textured wax to give it some shine.

Takashi Kurihara

担当スタイリスト
栗原 貴史
PEEK-A-BOO 原宿店 トップスタイリスト

Naoki "SAND" Yamamoto (SAND GRAPHICS)

03

デザイナー／ペインター

1979年生まれ、東京都在住。フリーデザイナーとしてグラフィックデザインをベースに活動。グラフィックレーベル「SAYHELLO」のほか、ペインターとして参加しているペインティング集団「81 BASTARDS」ではLAで個展を行うなど精力的に活動中。
www.sandgraphicstokyo.com ／ www.sayhellotokyo.com

Born in 1979. Naoki lives in Tokyo. He is freelance designer who majored in graphics. He works at the graphic label "SAYHELLO" and is part of a painting group "81 BASTARDS". He has also held a solo exhibition in LA.

一問一答 Question&Answer

Q PEEK-A-BOOに通ってどれくらいですか？
A 10年くらいです
Q どれくらいの頻度で通っているのですか？
A 月に1度くらい。友達に会いに行く感覚で行ってます

Q 中上さんの印象を教えてください
A 先輩だけど友達のような優しいお兄さん、かな（笑）
Q 髪型を決めるとき、何か参考にしていますか？
A 特にありません。最初に中上さんに相談して、ずっとこの髪型です

Q How did you find out about to PEEK-A-BOO?
A Almost ten years.
Q How often do you go?
A Once a month. It's like visiting friends.

Q What is your impression of Mr.Nakagami?
A He teaches me a lot but at the same time he's just like a friend and an older brother.
Q What influences you when you choose a new hairstyle?
A Nothing special. I asked him first time and now I keep having this style.

約7cmのレイヤーカットに質感が軽めのパーマをかけた、外国人のようなハードなクセ毛風スタイルです。スケートやピストカルチャーを通ってきた本人のライフスタイルやキャラクターがあってこそ成り立ちます。またスタイリングは乾かしてドライ系のクリームを少しなじませるだけでOKです。キャップを被ってもバランスよくまとまりますよ。

This style is inspired by very curly hair that some foreigners have, lightly perming his 7cm layered cut hair. Also his lifestyle involves skating and "pist culture" and this completes his character. For styling you just put a small amount of dry finishing cream on your hair after it gets dry. Wearing a cap makes it look well balanced too.

Makoto Nakaue

担当スタイリスト
中上 眞
PEEK-A-BOO 原宿店 ディレクター・店長

04

MADEMOISELLE YULIA

DJ／デザイナー／シンガー

1987年生まれ。10代のころから DJ を始め、ジャンルに捉われないオリジナルな選曲やパフォーマンスに注目が集まり、自身の手掛けるブランド「GIZA」のデザイナーの他、モデルとしても活動中。さらには、現在、シンガーとしてのシングル「GOGO/THIS WEEKEND」が iTunes などで発売中。yulia.tokyo/yulia

Born in 1987,YULIA started DJing when she was a teenager. She focuses on her performance and original selections that aren't limited by genre. She also works as a designer for her original brand "GIZA" and as a model. Further more, her single "GOGO/THIS WEEKEND" is now on iTunes.

一問一答 Question&Answer

Q PEEK-A-BOO に通ってどれくらいですか？
A 父が PEEK-A-BOO の美容師なので、生まれたときから、かな（笑）
Q PEEK-A-BOO 以外の美容室に通ったことは？
A ありません
Q ヘアカラーをブルー系にしたきっかけは？
A 最初は赤系のカラーにしていたのですが、そこから寒色系に変えたくて紫にして1年、その後で青にしました。もう青にして7年くらいになるのですが、イメージが定着してしまってなかなか変えられない状態です（笑）
Q やってみたい髪色は？
A シルバーかブロンド、黒もやりたいです

Q How long have you been coming to PEEK-A-BOO?
A ISince I was born. My father is a hairstylist at PEEK-A-BOO.
Q Have you ever been to any other hair salon except for PEEK-A-BOO?
A No
Q What made you decide to dye your hair blue?
A HAt first my hair was reddish but since I wanted to make it to cold color, I tried purple. One year later I had it dyed blue. It's been blue now for almost seven years but now everyone has an image of me with that color so I can't change…
Q What color do you want to try?
A Silver or blond, also black.

TOKYO HAIR

> ユリアさんはオシャレだし自分をしっかり持っていて本当に素敵な女性です。今回のヘアスタイルをマネするなら、カールがキープできるようなスプレーをしてからコテで巻いてください。また髪色がキレイに見えるように、オイルやグロススプレーを多めにつけるのもポイントです。ウェットに仕上げるときはグロスジュレを使っています。

Aya Yoshimi

担当スタイリスト
吉見 彩

PEEK-A-BOO 原宿店 スタイリスト

YULIA is fashionable, independent and a very nice woman. If you try this hairstyle, first apply some spray that helps your hair to keep curled then use a hair iron. You can also put some extra oil and glossy spray so that the hair color stands out. If you want to make it look wet, use glossy gel.

05 竹中 碧
女優／モデル

1987年生まれ。プラチナムプロダクション所属。北海道でモデルとしてキャリアをスタート。ファッションショーや雑誌などで活躍後、拠点を東京へ。現在は、女優としてテレビドラマやCMなど、徐々に活動の幅を広げる。今後の活躍から目が離せない注目株だ。

Born in 1987. Takenaka belongs to Platinum Production. She has developed her carrier as model in TV dramas and commercials. She's an upcoming star that you should keep an eye on.

一問一答 Question&Answer

Q どれくらいの頻度でPEEK-A-BOOに通っていますか？
A 1ヶ月半に1回ほどです
Q ヘアスタイルの参考にするモノはありますか？
A 街の人や雑誌を参考にします

Q How often do you go to PEEK-A-BOO?
A Every six weeks.
Q What influences you when you choose a new hairstyle?
A People I see about town and in magazines.

Q どんな時にヘアスタイルを変えたくなりますか？
A 素敵なヘアスタイルの人を見た時
Q チャレンジしてみたいヘアスタイルは？
A 黒髪のショートにしたい

Q When do you feel like changing your hairstyles?
A HWhen I see someone with a nice hairstyle.
Q What color do you want to try?
A Short black hair.

竹中さんは、綺麗なロングヘアが印象的なので、それを生かして長さをキープしながら、フェイスラインに少し表情が出るようにカットしています。重めなスタイリング剤を避けて、軽めのキープスプレーのみで仕上げるのもポイントですね。

She has beautiful long hair so I try to make use of it, keeping its length and expressing nuances around her face. The best way to set this style is using spray lightly. Avoid heavy texture.

Takuyoshi Nishio

担当スタイリスト
西尾 卓義
PEEK-A-BOO 原宿店 シニアスタイリスト・副店長

part 5

HISTORY of HAIR STYLE

コシノジュンコ × 川島文夫の
ヘアスタイル談義

30年以上前から交友のあるファッションデザイナー・コシノジュンコ氏と
PEEK-A-BOO代表・川島文夫氏。
2人が現在まで見てきたヘアとファッションについて、
ざっくばらんに教えてもらった。

Junko Koshino x Fumio Kawashima Hair style discussion

Designer Ms. Junko Koshino and PEEK-A-BOO founder Mr. Fumio kawashima; we asked about hair and fashion throughout their friendship for over 30 years.

ーまずはお２人の出会いから教えてください。

川島：僕はロンドンの Vidal Sassoon で勉強をした後、'70年代後半に日本に帰ってきたのですが、共通の友人を介してジュンコ先生を紹介してもらったんです。

コシノ：私は元々ロンドンの音楽やファッションが好きだったので、PEEK-A-BOOがロンドンの空気とヘアを日本に持ってきたものだから、待ってましたといった感じでした。

川島：実際、ジュンコ先生はとっても暖かく迎えてくれました。

- How did you two know each other?

Kawashima : After I studied in "Vidal Sassoon" in London, I came back to Japan in late 70's. What was when I first met her through a mutual friend.

Koshino : I always liked music and fashion culture in London so when he brought the London style beauty aesthetes, I was like "yes!"

Kawashima : Yes, she actually welcomed me with open arms.

コシノ：だってファッションって洋服だけでは完成しないでしょう？ヘアとメイクでいかようにも変化するんです。ヘアメイク抜きにしてファッションショーは成り立たないですから。

川島：そうですね。今はヘアとファッション抜きには、生活自体もできないんじゃないかな。

コシノ：衣食住に足りないのは"遊"。遊びココロがないと前に進まないし全然面白くないわよね。もっと面白いことをやりたいわね、一緒に。

川島：ぜひやりたいですね！ジュンコ先生の洋服は、シャープでジオメトリックで僕の作る髪型と重なる部分がかなりあると思うんです。それは出会った当時も今も変わりません。ちなみにPEEK-A-BOOがオープンした時に、ジュンコ先生がトレーナーのデザインをしてくださったんです。グリーンのトレーナーに刺繍が入っていて、すごくカッコよかったんですよ。

コシノ：まず男しかいない美容室って革命的だったわよね。当時の美容室は白衣を着たおばさんがいるイメージだったけれど、フレッシュでかわいい男の子たちが揃っていて、PEEK-A-BOOに行くとモードを感じられたんです。

川島：ちょうどロンドンのテイストと東京の雰囲気がうまくミックスされたんですよね。

Koshino : Beauty takes a huge part of Fashion you know? Garment cannot complete fashion by itself and beauty can give various finish to it.

Kawashima : That is true. We may not be able to live without both fashion and hair.

Koshino : What's missing in human life's principal "Clothes, Food, Home" is "Play". We have to have wit and humor, otherwise there's no progress and what's worth it? I think we should "play" more.

Kawashima : That'd be wonderful. I think those geometric and sharp impression you create in your design somewhat relates to my style of hair creation. I had this feeling when I saw your design and I still do. Oh, and I loved your design for PEEK-A-BOO's opening. It was really cool green sweatshirt with embroideries.

Koshino : Is was quite evolutionary to see a hair salon with all male employees. Back then, the stable image for hair salon was an old lady with white lab coat, but PEEK-A-BOO fresh boys brought "mode" and fashionable feels to the industry.

Kawashima : I think it was a good timing for mixing up London influence into Tokyo culture.

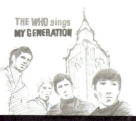

コシノ：PEEK-A-BOOに行くと誰もがカッコよくなったものね。髪を切ることで人生を変えられた人はたくさんいると思うわよ。

川島：ありがとうございます。実際、お店に来てくれた人たちはチャレンジが好きな人ばかりだったので、お互いに共鳴できたんだと思います。

コシノ：でも本当にすごく発展しましたね。今や世界に通じる美容界の大スターですよ。

川島：今、こうしていられるのも'70年代にジュンコ先生と知り合うことができて、良い仲間が青山にいたお陰です。

Koshino : It was quite obvious that everyone looked so much better when they go to PEEK-A-BOO. I'm sure you guys changed so many people's lives for that.

Kawashima : That's so nice of you to say. I actually think our customers came to us because they were looking for something new or not afraid of changing, so it worked for both of us.

Koshino : But you guys grow impressively. You definitely are crowned as a big star in this industry.

Kawashima : that is all because of you and my people around me. I am so lucky to know you back in the day and have supporting friends in Aoyama.

ー常に第一線で活躍されるお2人ですが、これからの夢はありますか？

コシノ：2020年には東京オリンピック・パラリンピックがあります。私も文化・教育委員をしていますが、舞台が東京とはいえこのオリンピック・パラリンピックは日本のオリンピック・パラリンピックです。日本中が日本の文化を世界にアピールすることができる絶好の機会です。先日、京都国立博物館にて琳派400周年を記念し「能とファッション」をテーマにファッションショーを行いました。無視することのできない日本の伝統文化を現代にどう生かしていくかが課題です。

川島：僕はユニバーサルデザインの髪型を作りたいんです。切られる人の顔型や髪質の違いで仕上がりは別のものに見えるけど、実は1つのテクニックで作られている、というのがやりたいんですよ。

ーお2人のますますのご活躍に期待しております！

- You both have been leaders for each industries, how do you foresee yourselves in the future? Any dreams?

Koshino : I am a member of culture/education committee for Tokyo Olympic/Paralympic in 2020, and very excited for this opportunity to showcase culture of not only Tokyo but this whole country. I recently directed this fashion show in Kyoto with the theme of "Nou (能) meets Fashion." My goal is to preserve Japanese cultural heritage.

Kawashima : I want to do a conceptual thing like, a universal hair design. I'd like to make one hairstyle using the same exact techniques for different facial features. It should look different but the cut is the same.

- Well, both of your projects sound so much fun!

コシノ氏の人生が綴られた『COLLECTION』（右）と、'70年代の原宿で撮られた写真をまとめた『70' HARAJUKU』（左）。『70' HARAJUKU』の中には若き日のコシノ氏の写真も収められている。

コシノジュンコ / Junko Koshino

文化服装学院在学中に新人デザイナーの登竜門・装苑賞を最年少の19歳で受賞。1978年パリコレクション初参加。世界各地にてショーを開催。オペラやブロードウェイミュージカルの舞台衣装、スポーツユニフォーム、インテリアデザイン等、幅広く活動。

Jonko Koshino won So-en Prize (known as a gateway to success for a new fashion designer) at the age of 19 as the youngest winner in history while studying in Bunka Fashion College. She directs fashions shows around the world ever since. She also does costumes design for operas and broadways, design for sports uniform, and interior design.

川島文夫 / Fumio Kawashima

1971年にロンドンのVidal Sassoonに参加し、1975年にボックスボブを生み出し世界中から注目を集める。同年に帰国し1977年、表参道にPEEK-A-BOOをオープン。以後、時代をリードし続ける。

Joined Vidal Sassoon in London in 1971. He created "Box bob" in 1975 and it became a great sensation in all over the world. He flew back to Japan in the same year and opened PEEK-A-BOO salon in Omotesando in 1977. He has been leading the industry ever since.

(R) "COLLECTION" tells about Ms. Koshino's life story.
(L) "70' HARAJUKU" is a photo book about Harajuku in 70's.

part
6

HAIR
ORDER
LIST

なりたいヘアスタイルを
実現するためのオーダーリスト

なりたいヘアスタイルを作るためには、
どのようにオーダーすれば良いのか。
ここでは、5つのなりたい髪型をピックアップし、
作り方のコツをカットとスタイリングのポイントから解説。

Find the style to be who you wanna be.

Let us show you how to order your desirable hair.
We picked 5 styles and tips for maintain.

 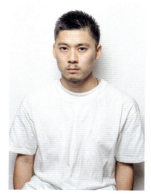 

Order List.1
(とにかく好印象な
ヘアスタイルを作りたい)
P102~P103

Order List.2
(セットに時間を
掛けたくない)
P104~P105

Order List.3
(パーマスタイルに
チャレンジしたい)
P106~P107

Order List.4
(個性的なスタイルに
挑戦したい)
P108~P109

Order List.5
(クールで女性らしい
スタイルにしたい)
P110~P111

Order List.1
とにかく好印象な
ヘアスタイルを作りたい
Hairstyle for best impression.

Style.01

適度の刈り上げと毛流れを意識
Clean shaving and smooth flow.

ツヤと毛束感が感じられる、大人っぽいサイドパートのヘアスタイル。額を出すのも好印象に見せるポイントの1つだ。スタイリングは、ジェルを馴染ませた後に手ぐしで整えるだけでOK。簡単に作れる好印象スタイルだ。

model：Ryusei

Cut Point

サイドを少し刈り上げて、
スッキリさせるのがポイント

Shaved side sihoulette for cleanliness.

Recommend Styling

下から上に髪全体をジェルで
馴染ませるように付ける

Apply hair gel upwards lightly and entirely.

model：Ryo

Cut Point

耳周りや襟足などは
スッキリさせつつも
刈り上げすぎないのがポイント

Temples and necklines should be clean yet kept enough thickness.

Recommend Styling

オイルワックスを内側から
中間毛先にしっかり付けて
手ぐしで後方にとかす

Apply oil wax from the inside towards the halfway to the tip of your hair firmly and comb towards back with your hand.

Style.02

黒髪 & センター分けの王道スタイル

Clean shaving and smooth flow.

目鼻立ちがハッキリしている人は、髪を短くツンツンさせるより、毛流れが表現できるスタイルにすると好印象な雰囲気に。サイドパートより、センターパートにすることで、より爽やかな印象を作ることが可能だ。

Order List.2

セットに時間を掛けたくない

Time-saving hairstyle.

model：Ryuzo

Cut Point

頭の形に合わせグラデーションになるように刈り上げる

Shave the hair by changing the length gradually along the head shape.

Recommend Styling

グリースをさっと付けるだけでスタイリングが完成する

Just apply hair grease.

Style.01

計算されたミニマムさが手軽さを生む

Well thought minimal hair is easy to set.

シンプルな分、カットのクオリティが鍵を握るヘアスタイル。トップだけを残し、グラデーションのバランスを保つのが大事なポイント。ドライヤーもいらず、簡単にスタイリングをできるのがメリットだ。

Style.02
フォルムを整えたシンプルヘア
Simple and clean shaped hair.

カットの段階でしっかりと形を整えておけば、必然的に
セットもスムーズに。コメカミ部分などのアウトラインを
スッキリさせれば、美しいフォルムを作ることができる。
直毛の人は、少しパーマをかけるのもオススメ。

Cut Point

アウトラインを刈り上げて、
グラデーションになるように整える

Shave the outline and smoothen
the length.

Recommend Styling

リーゼントスタイルをイメージし、
ジェルを揉み込んで縦長シルエットに

Firmly apply hair gel to make
vertical (pompadour) silhouette.

model : Daisuke

Order List.3
パーマスタイルに
チャレンジしたい
Trying a permed style.

Style.01

クセ毛風パーマでワイルドに
Wild natural curly hair.

クセ毛風パーマは、欧米人のような雰囲気が生まれ、大人っぽい印象に。パーマがかかっている分、アンダーセクションを甘めに刈り上げ、オーバーセクションはマッシュベースのひし形フォルムでスッキリ見せるのもポイントだ。

Perme Point

髪の毛を濡らし、
タオルドライでカールを活かす

wet the hair and wipe with towel to maximize the curl.

Recommend Styling

ジェルでオールバックにスタイリング

Apply hair gel and pull back the hair.

model : Ryosuke

model：Yasuhiro

Perme Point

複数のロッドをランダムに巻き、
動きのあるヘアスタイルを作る

Winding the rood to random
to give active look.

Recommend Styling

濡らした髪を自然乾燥後、
毛先にムースを揉み込めばOK

Naturally dry the hair
and apply hair mousse onto the tips.

Style.02

アシンメトリーな
パーマスタイルで大人っぽく

Asymmetry and mature prem style.

ミディアムのレングスでアシンメトリーにスタイリングするのがポイント。片方を耳に掛けることで落ち着いた雰囲気を作り、顔周りに表情が生まれるため、大人っぽいパーマスタイルが完成する。

Order List.4

個性的なスタイルに挑戦したい

Unique hairstyles.

model:Tatsumasa

Cut Point

バリカンで骨格に合わせて
グラデーションを作る
Shave along the facial outline.

Recommend Styling

ウェットでもマットな
スタイリングでもOK
Works both for wet or dry look.

Style.01
着こなしと合わせて個性的に
Balance with your outfit and make it one if a kind.

アシンメトリーのモヒカンスタイルは、ミニマムなフォルムとセパレートしたカラーリングが特徴。個性の強いシャツなどと合わせても十分にハマるヘアスタイルだ。洋服に合わせてスタイリングを変えられるのも楽しみの1つ。

Style.02
顔立ちに合わせて前髪ラインを設定
Create best bangs line for your face feature.

アンダーセクションはバリカンで刈り上げてスッキリと見せる。目力がより強調されるように、前髪をギリギリのラインで整えるのがポイント。グリースを付けて、最後にブラシで毛流れを作ると、より綺麗なラインが作れる。

Cut Point

前下がりでナチュラルな
毛流れをつくるようにカットする

Cut the front part longer
and make flow to the silhouette.

Recommend Styling

髪の内側からグリースを
揉み込むように馴染ませる

Apply hair grease from inside firmly.

model : Hiromitsu

Order List.5

クールで女性らしい
スタイルにしたい

Cool feminine style.

Style.01

立体感が鍵を握るショートカット

Solid and architectural short cut.

前下がりのショートスタイルは、カットの角度で作るグラデーションが肝。あごのラインに沿って作り上げれば、綺麗なシルエットが生まれる。角度を付ける分、スタイリングはふんわりボリュームを出して、女性らしさをキープしたい。

model：Peace

Cut Point

立体感が生まれるよう、
角度を付けてカット
Cut with angles for solidify look.

Recommend Styling

ドライパウダーで
ふんわりとしたシルエットを作る
Apply dry powder
for soft impression and silhouette.

model：Mei

Cut Point

前下がりのシルエットを作るために
バックはスッキリとしたラインに

Give clean cut for the neckline
and extend to the longer front part.

Recommend Styling

シアバターとヘアオイルで
セミウェットな質感を作る

Use sheer butter and hair oil
for semi-wet texture.

Style.02

ボブスタイルで作る
クール & フェミニンスタイル

Cool & feminine bob hair.

ボブスタイルは、いつの時代もキマる定番スタイルだ。柔らかいパーマを加えることで、クールさの中に女性らしい雰囲気もプラスできる。カラーリングを変えたり、パーマを変えたりと表情の変化も楽しめるヘアスタイルだ。

part
7

HOW TO MAKE BEST HAIR

理想のヘアスタイルを
作るためのお悩み Q&A

ヘアスタイルにまつわるあらゆることを Q&A 形式でご紹介。
理想のヘアスタイルを作るために必要な、
11 つのクエスチョンとアンサー。

Q&A for Your Hair Concerns

11 topics and answers to guide you the best hair styles.

Question. 1

Q 自分に合ったヘアスタイルの見つけ方は？
How can I find my ideal hair style?

A 顔の形に合わせてヘアスタイルを選ぶのがポイント
Choose a style based on your facial contours.

自分の顔の形に合わせてヘアスタイルをセレクトすれば、
すんなりと馴染む好印象なスタイルが作れるハズ。
Different face shape has different styles to outshine.

Long Face _ 面長

顔の横に重さを持たせたりマッシュショートなどの、丸みのあるスタイルが◎。ポイントはパーマで丸みのある質感とフォルムにし、ひし形シルエットに近づけること。

Spuare Face _ 四角顔

エラが張った四角い輪郭の人は、前下がりでAラインのボブスタイルがマッチする。うまく輪郭をカバーすることが可能で、毛先にパーマをかければ、よりソフトで優しい印象に。

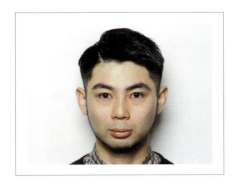

Round Face _ 丸顔

丸顔の輪郭の人は、マッシュルームカットなどの丸く見えてしまうカットは避けたい。少し縦長のひし形シルエットに近づけるのがオススメで、刈り上げスタイルが好相性。

Inverted Triangle Face _ 逆三角顔

アゴが細くて華奢なイメージの逆三角形の輪郭の人は、前上がりのマッシュショートやステップカット等の奥行きのあるフォルムにすると、顔の形をうまくカバーすることが可能だ。

HARD

ARMINDO BS STYLING FREEZ KEEP GEL

ツヤとホールド感が特徴のジェル。シトラスティーアロマの香りも◎。1500円+税（200g／アリミノ）

ARIMINO PEACE PRODESIGN SERIES FREEZE KEEP WAX

立体的な束感が作れるワックス。カシスのスッキリとした香りが特徴。1500円+税（40g／アリミノ）

MILBON PREJUME WAX 7

しっかりとしたセット力で、すぐには固まらないマットな質感を生む。1300円+税（90g／株式会社ミルボン）

MILBON QUFRA VOLUME KEEP SPRAY

ホールド感が特徴のボリュームキープスプレー。フルーティフローラルの香り。1600円+税（175g／株式会社ミルボン）

GLOSS ← → **MAT**

FINE COSMETICS CHARMING POMADE

ツヤ感が楽しめるポマード。何度もセットし直すことが可能だ。1500円+税（210g／FINE COSMETICS）

VILLA LODOLA LIBER WAX

自然なツヤとウェットな質感が特徴。柔らかなスタイリングを可能にする。2300円+税（50ml／株式会社ミルボン）

SHISEIDO STAGE WORKS POWDER SHAKE

髪を動かしたい人にオススメ。適度なボリューム感を楽しめる。1500円+税（150ml／資生堂プロフェッショナル株式会社）

DAVINES MORE INSIDE NINO POWDER HAIR WAX

自然なスタイルを生むパウダーワックス。揉み込むようにスタイリング。2600円+税（8g／株式会社コンフォートジャパン）

SOFT

Question. 2

自分に合ったスタイリング剤の選び方は？
How do I choose my hair styling products?

作り上げたいヘアスタイルを決めて、ベストなスタイリング剤をセレクト
It varies on the hair style. There are best products for each style and finish.

数多の商品がラインナップするスタイリング剤。
ここでは、グラフ形式でオススメの商品をご紹介。
Our recommendations for each style with specifications.

Question. 3

 簡単に見た目の印象を変えるには？
I wanna have an easy / quick makeover.

 分け目、毛流れを変えて印象チェンジ
giving a different parting can change an impression.

いつものスタイリングに飽きてしまったという人にオススメな、簡単アレンジサンプルをご紹介。
Hair style samples for avoiding your tedious hair.

Center Part
_ センター・パート

正統派な印象のセンター分けのヘアスタイル。スタイングは、前髪を左右対象にすることと、ウェット系のスタイリング剤でツヤを出せば、モードで知的なスタイルが完成する。

Side Part
_ サイド・パート

社交的で柔らかい印象のサイドパートスタイル。ビジネスシーンにもピッタリなヘアスタイル。スタイリングポイントは、眉頭から眉山の間にパートを付けること。ワックスで柔らかく外ハネを意識しよう。

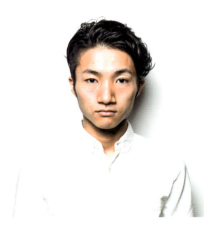

Off the face
_ オフ・ザ・フェイス

アクティヴでワイルドな印象が作れるオールバックのヘアスタイル。ジェルやグリースを髪全体に馴染ませツヤツヤに仕上げよう。手ぐしでかき上げるだけの簡単スタイルが完成する。

Question. 4

 直毛の悩みを解決するには？
My hair is so stubbornly straight.

 パーマスタイルで簡単に洒落感がプラスできる
Try permed styles! that is just as easy as that.

日本人ならではの悩みである直毛。そんな時はパーマスタイルが最適だ。
今、オススメのパーマスタイルをご紹介。

Straight hair can be a boring feature for many Japanese fellows.
Here are some suggestions for permed styles.

Soft Curly Perm
_ ソフトカーリーパーマ

欧米風の雰囲気を作り上げるソフトカーリーパーマ。季節を問わず、アクティヴな印象が感じられるオススメなヘアスタイルだ。

Spiral Perm
_ スパイラルパーマ

直毛かつロングヘアの人にはラテン系のスパイラルパーマがオススメ。スタイリングいらずで作れる楽チンパーマスタイル。

Short Dread Perm
_ ショートドレッドパーマ

難易度が高めだが、インパクトのあるショートドレッドパーマもオススメ。ブラックカルチャーが感じられる、人気のパーマスタイルだ。

Hot Carl Perm
_ ホットカールパーマ

女性にオススメなのが、50'sテイストのセクシーなホットカールパーマ。全体に柔らかい質感を出すことで、アヴァンギャルドな印象に。

Question. 5

 もみあげのベストな長さは？
How far should I grow my sideburns?

 耳の2/3の長さに設定するのがベスト
To the 2/3 of your ear length.

濃さに個人差があるもみあげ。"2/3"の長さを意識するだけで、全体のバランスがぐっと良くなる。

Even the thickness varies, the length of "two-thirds" gives the balanced to hair and facial outlines.

長すぎると、野暮ったいイメージになり、短すぎるとフェイスラインが強調され過ぎてしまう。

耳の長さの2/3にすることでフェイスラインが整い、ヘアスタイル全体が好バランスに。

Question. 6

 シャンプーの正しいやり方は？
What is the proper method of washing my hair?

 基本に忠実に。手間を惜しまず丁寧さを意識
Stick to the basics; thoroughly and gently.

予洗い、泡立て、しっかり流すという基本に改めて着目してみよう。

Prewash, lather, rinse off are the basic rules.

Step.01

毛穴の汚れをしっかりと落とすには38度くらいのお湯で予洗い。予洗いすることで、余分な汚れが落ち、シャンプー時の泡立ちがアップする。

To cleanse your scalp throughly, 30 degree is the best temperature of the water. Prewash helps deeper cleansing and richer lather.

Step.02

500円玉ほどの量を取る。直接シャンプー剤を頭皮に付けるのではなく、手のひらで軽く泡立ててから髪に馴染ませる。

Take the liquid on your hands and whisk lightly in your hands before apply onto your hair.

Step.03

頭皮に負担をかけないように、爪を立てたり必要以上にゴシゴシ洗うのはやめよう。指の腹を使ってマッサージするように洗うのが◎。

Wash and lather with your finger cushion as if massaging your head. Do not scratch your scalp with your nails to stress both your hair and scalp.

Step.04

シャンプーのすすぎ残しは、毛穴詰まりの原因となるのでしっかりと流す。

Rinse throughly to avoid solution clogged on your scalp.

Question. 7

Q ドライヤーのかけ方のコツは？
What is the tips for using a hair dryer?

A スタイリングの土台として"風"を利用する
Use the "breeze" for the foundation of hair styling.

ドライヤーは、ただ乾かすためだけでなく、次のステップであるスタイリングの土台として考えよう。
When using a hair dryer, take the blowing not only to dry your hair. It sets the base to style your hair.

Point.01

髪を軽く濡らした後、ドライヤーの強風を地肌に当てる。その際、しっかりと手を振ることで根元のクセを取ることができる。

Most your hair lightly and blow the dryer twards the scalp. Swing your hands in your hair to help smoother flow of your hair.

Point.02

指で髪をひっぱりドライヤーの熱を当てる。その後、冷風で冷ますことで、さらにクセを伸ばすことも可能だ。

Pull your hair gently and use the dryer. After drying with heated blow, you can straighten your hair with using cold blowing.

Point.03

トップにボリュームを出したい場合、ブラシで根元を起こし、ドライヤーの熱を根元に向けて当てるのがポイント。

Using hair brush and give the dryer's heat to the roots well help maximizing your hair volume.

Question. 8

Q 髪のケア方法は？
How should I care my hair?

A 髪の毛の健康には頭皮のケアが鍵
Well treated scalp is the key to the healthy hair.

頭皮の状態に合ったシャンプー、トリートメントを使えば、生き生きとした髪の毛へ。
Choose the best shampoo and conditioner for your hair condition.

頭皮の状態を知ろう

皮脂や汗をそのままにしていると、毛穴につまり酸化するため、匂いやかゆみ、フケ、抜け毛の原因に。また、乾燥したままの状態にしておくと、肌の老化が3倍のスピードで進むとも言われている。

 オイリーな頭皮

 乾燥した頭皮

 正常な頭皮

対処方法

頭皮の状態に合わせたシャンプーを選んで、頭皮を健康に保つ。

for OILY scalp

DAVINES NATURALTECH SHAMPOO (R)

頭皮の匂いやベタつきを改善してくれるシャンプー。スッキリサラサラヘアに。2200円＋税（250ml／株式会社コンフォートジャパン）

for DRY scalp

DAVINES NATURALTECH SHAMPOO (W)

乾燥した頭皮に潤いを与え、ふんわりとしたまとまりやすい髪へ導く。2200円＋税（250ml／株式会社コンフォートジャパン）

for Scalp treatment

KERASTASE SP SERUM SENSIDOTE

頭皮バランスを整え健康な状態へと導く、洗い流さないスカルプトリートメント。3500円＋税（50ml／ケラスターゼ）

Question.9

 ヘアカラーを長持ちさせるには？
How can I keep my hair color?

 しっかりとしたケアを心掛けよう
Your hair color lasts with a proper care.

カラーを長持ちさせるには、専用のケア用品を用いれば、よりカラーを持続することが可能だ。
Choose hair care products for colored hair.

原因

褪色（ヘアカラーの色落ち）の原因は、毎日のシャンプーや紫外線、ドライヤーの熱など様々だ。カラーリング直後の髪は、キューティクルに隙間ができてしまうため、シャンプーをした時に、泡や水と一緒に色素が流れ出てしまい褪色が進んでしまう。

解決方法 01

褪色を防ぐには、弱酸性や、アミノ酸を主成分としたシャンプーの使用をオススメ。
Weak-acidic or amino-acidic shampoo will delay fading your hair color.

KERASTASE RF BAIN CHROMA RICHE
傷んだ髪を整え、褪色を抑えながら潤いを与える。2800円+税（250ml／ケラスターゼ）

解決方法 02

カラーシャンプーなどを使用して、流れ出た色素を補充してあげるという方法も。
Colored conditioner can restore faded pigment to your hair.

ANAP COLOR SHAMPOO VIOLET
アッシュ系などのカラーの色持ちさせるのに最適なシャンプー。2600円+税（200ml／ANAP）

Question.10

 雨の日でもヘアスタイルをキメルには？
How can I maintain my hair on a rainy day?

 湿気に負けない髪の毛をつくることが重要
Create damage-less hair to even shine in moisture-laden air.

雨の日の湿気でうねりがちの髪の毛は、トリートメントで補修して解決。
Use hair treatment to prevent fuzzy hair by a rainy day moist.

原因

雨の日にスタイリングが決まらないのは、髪の毛のダメージによるもの。キューティクルが剥がれた部分から水分を吸収してしまい、その部分が膨張してうねりを起こす。

解決方法

髪の内部に栄養が行きわたるように、トリートメントでケアをしてあげること。栄養が詰まっている状態にすれば、髪内部に湿気が侵入する場所がなくなり、クセが出づらくなる。

DEARTECH UKUWA
湿気に強い皮膜を形成し、湿気をブロック。1日中スタイルをキープするトリートメント。1800円+税（100g／DEARTECH）

Question. 11

Q ヘアスタイルと相性の良い
アイウエアは？
Are there any hairstyles look good with eyewear?

A 歴代のスタイルアイコンを
参考にしよう
Let's see the style icons in the history.

ヘアスタイルとアイウエアのベストマッチの関係を探る。
Finding the best-matched pairs of hair styles and eyewear.

John Lennon
_ ジョン・レノン

UK Layer Short ✕ Round Frame

サイドを長めに残したUKらしさ感じるヘアスタイルのジョン・レノン。ニュアンスのあるパーマには、ラウンドフレームのアイウエアが柔らかい印象をプラス。昨今人気のラウンドフレームとの組み合わせは、ぜひ参考にして欲しい。

Jonny Depp
_ ジョニー・デップ

Short Bob ✕ Smoke Lens

ラフにバッグへかき上げたヘアに、スモークレンズのサングラスを組み合わせたワイルドなスタイルのジョニー・デップ。ショートレングスをキープすることで、より大人な雰囲気を演出することが可能なオススメスタイルだ。

Kurt Cobain
_ カート・コバーン

Grunge Bob ✕ Fox Type

カート・コバーンを象徴するグランジボブとフォックス型のサングラスの組み合わせも鉄板だ。ランダムに見せたセンターパートのヘアスタイルに、インパクトのあるサングラスで個性的なスタイルが完成する。

Tommy Guerrero
_ トミー・ゲレロ

Wavy Short ✕ Square Frame

ショートヘアで作るパーマスタイルに、スクエアのサングラスを合わせたトミー・ゲレロ。柔らかいイメージのヘアスタイルと、角ばったアイウエアのギャップが好バランスを生む。額を出すことで大人っぽい印象をプラスする。

Ryuichi Sakamoto
_ 坂本 龍一

Center Part ✕ Boston Frame

坂本龍一といえば、センターパートのヘアスタイルとボストンフレームのアイウエアが印象的。定番的なセンターパートに、丸みが特徴のボストンタイプがクラシックな雰囲気を生み出す。モノトーンの色味を作り上げている点も注目したい。

Twiggy
_ ツイッギー

Tight Short ✕ Big Round

ツイッギーの代名詞とも言えるショートヘアに、インパクトのあるビックフレームサングラスの組み合わせ。ゴールドベージュ系の髪色を生かして、フレームにも色味を取り入れた上級者スタイルだ。ポップさを併せ持つ雰囲気も◎。

Part 8
SEVEN MUST TOOLS

TOKYO HAIRを支える、7つの神器

スタイリストたちの技術を支える7つの道具をピックアップ。
細部にまでこだわり抜いて作られた神器と呼ぶべき道具の魅力を、
余すことなくお見せしよう。

The seven sacred tools for TOKYO HAIR.

Introducing the seven tools, which could even be called sacred to the stylists.

01.Scissors

スタイリストにとって、最も身近にあり最も大切な道具がシザー。PEEK-A-BOOでは持ったときのフィット感や切れ味など、徹底的にこだわり抜いて作られたシザーを全スタイリストが用いている。髪型のベースを作るカットシザー（左）は、熟練した職人が手仕事で仕上げる究極の1本と呼ぶにふさわしい仕上がりだ。ブラントカットに最適な特殊な銅を用いており、ソフトな切れ味が長い間持続するのも嬉しいところ。一方、毛量を調整するセニングシザー（右）は、厚い毛束をスムーズに削ぐことができるよう刃先の山を深く加工しているのが特徴。キレのある抜け感とパワーのある切れ味が実現できると評判なのだ。

Needless to say that the scissors are the essential to any hair stylist, and the ones used in PEEK-A-BOO's stylists' hands are extremely well made. The cutting scissors were made with special copper created by artisanal techniques. The material is perfect for blunt cutting and has long lasting sharpness while thinning scissors have deeper depth on the blades for smooth and powerful cutting.

02.Brush

美しいヘアスタイルを仕上げるのに必要なブラシは、なりたいイメージによって使い分けるのが重要。熱に強く、抗菌性に優れたセラミックピンブラシ（右）は、髪通りがスムーズな上にドライヤーの熱にも強いので、ヘビーデューティなサロンワークでの強い味方。さらにソフトなベースラバーを用いることで、ふんわり柔らかな仕上がりが簡単に実現できる。目の粗いスケルトンブラシ（左）は、トップにボリュームを出したり、毛流れをつけたいときに最適。ジェルを付けたあとでなめす、ジェルパックの際にも髪がペッタリせず自然に仕上がるのでオススメ。静電気が起こりにくく髪への負担が少ないのも特筆すべき点。

Different hairbrushes are used for different hair styles. This ceramic pin brush has high heat-resistance for heavy use with dryers in hair salons, and its soft rubber base can create whimsical silhouette for the styling. The skelton brush on the other hand, can give certain flow to the hair. It is also a great choice for combing gel styling without losing the volume of the hair. The likable features also include its hair-stress/electrostatic free material.

03.Sprayer

ヘアカットをスムーズに行うために欠かせないのが、スプレイヤーの存在だ。ブラックボディにホワイトのロゴがスタイリッシュなPEEK-A-BOOのスプレイヤーは、見た目の良さだけでなく機能面にもこだわりが凝縮されている。まず、日本製の高品質なヘッドを用いることで、きめが細かく均一な霧が生まれるのだ。さらに、小さい手でも扱いやすいようトップをスリムに、ボトムを雫型に設計しているのだと言う。どれを使っても同じだと感じてしまいがちだが、これは違う。サロンに置いておくだけでサマになるデザインと、あらゆるスタイリストのニーズを満たした、スプレイヤーの究極のカタチがここにある。

People may say what would be the difference in sprayers. Well, there are some thoughts behind this PEEK-A-BOO's stylish sprayer. Besides this appealing visual, PEEK-A-BOO uses this spray heads made in Japan, which make fine and even mist. The shape of the bottle also makes the workflow easier even with small hands. This is an ultimate sprayer for hair professionals.

04.Comb

ヘアスタイルの仕上がりを左右するコームは、隠れた名脇役。密歯とやや狭い粗歯を組み合わせたカットコーム（右）は、みねが程よくカーブしているので、頭にフィットしやすく、使い込むほどに手に馴染んでいく。長く尖った柄と細かなコームが組み合わさったテールコーム（左）は、耐薬品性に優れた素材と安定したグリップが特徴。安定したシェープとスライスができるので、ロッドを巻いたりアレンジをする際に活躍する。両方のコームとも、1cmごとにメモリが打ってあるので、長さの感覚が視覚でとらえやすいのも特筆すべきポイント。さらに、カラーバリエーションも豊富なので、お気に入りを見つける楽しさもある。

Combs will define the finish of hairstyles. This cut comb has two types of gaps in tooth and is slightly arced for accurate fitting to the curve of heads. The tail comb can give a stylist precise control in sectioning hair with its fine teeth and long tail. The material is durable for chemical use and has firm grip for stable use. Both types of comb have marks in every centimeter for practicing measurements and come in various colors for the stylists' choice.

05.Grease

ポマードのような濡れたツヤが出るクールグリースは、カッチリとしたショートヘアの仕上げに取り入れるべきスタイリング剤。初めて使う人は代名詞とも呼ぶべきクールグリースG（左）がオススメ。ウエット感、ツヤ、セット力のバランスが抜群で、ワックスなどの整髪料とミックスして使うのにも最適だ。クールグリースR（右）は朝作ったスタイルが1日中キープできる強めのセット力が魅力。さらにライム（クールグリースG）とアップル（クールグリースR）のフレッシュな香りが楽しめるのも人気の秘密。油性のポマードと違って水溶性だから、シャンプーで簡単に落とせて、デイリーに取り入れやすいのもオススメの理由。

Cool Grease is a perfect hair product for any clean short hair Look. Cool Grease G is an all-rounder for any users and can be mixed with hair wax for various wet'n' shiny finish while Cool Grease R can hold hair much firmer throughout the day. Cool Grease G has lime scent and Cool Grease R is scented with apple for pleasing use. Not like oily pomade, Cool Grease is water-soluble product, so much friendlier for daily uses.

06.Hair clipper

90年以上の歴史を持つアメリカの老舗ヘアクリッパーブランド・ウォールは、世界中のヘアスタイリストたちから愛され続けている。数ある名機の中から PEEK-A-BOO で使用しているのは、クロムスタイル・プロ（左）とクロミニ・プロ（右）。ドイツ製精密刃を用いたクロムスタイル・プロは、0.6mm から 3mm まで 5 段階の切り換えができ、とってもパワフル。ひとまわり小さなクロミニ・プロは、もみあげや襟足を整えるのにもってこい。この 2 機を上手く組み合わせることで、スタイルを作り上げていくというわけだ。さらに音が静かで振動が少ないストレスフリーな使い心地や、長時間使える容量の大きなバッテリーも魅力的。

WAHL brand's Chrome Style Pro and Chro-Mini Pro are PEEK-A-BOO's choice of their hair clippers. The long-standing of over 90 years, this American brand gained so much trust from hair stylists all over the world including those in PEEK-A-BOO. Chrome Style Pro has fine German blades and has range of length choice from 0.6mm to 3mm while Chro-Mini Pro is reliable for sideburns or hair line along the neck for accurate finish. Both models are designed to reduce noise and vibration for stress-free use and long-lasting battery.

07.Crocodile Clip

デザイン性の高さが目を引く、クリップの先端にあるワニの口のような折り返しが、ブロッキングしたい髪をしっかりキャッチしてくれるクロコダイルクリップ。硬い髪や長い髪はもちろん、濡れて重くなった髪でもすんなりと留めることができるので、1度使えば手放せなくなるという名品だ。さらにボディにはマットコーティングが施されているため、カラー剤やパーマ液などですべりやすくなっていても問題なく使えるという、サロンワークを考慮している点もポイントが高い。スムーズなサロンワークを進める上で、このクロコダイルクリップは必要不可欠な存在であることは間違いない！

Once you go with the crocodile clips, you cannot go back. The clip has this notch on its tip that hold hair firmly even if it's thick, long, wet or heavy. Also coated with matt finish so it won't slip off while using with any hair solutions. This clip is such an essential to all hair stylists for their professional work.

peek-a-boo

PEEK-A-BOO 青山
東京都港区青山 3-6-16 表参道サンケイビル 2F
03・5466・6311

PEEK-A-BOO 表参道
東京都渋谷区神宮前 4-3-15 東京セントラル 1F
03・3402・8214

PEEK-A-BOO ANNEX
東京都渋谷区神宮前 4-3-13 河野ビル 1F
03・5411・5421

PEEK-A-BOO オリンピア原宿
東京都渋谷区神宮前 6-35-3 コープオリンピア 1F
03・5468・5740

PEEK-A-BOO 原宿
東京都渋谷区神宮前 6-27-8 エムズ原宿 4F
03・5468・0822

GINZA PEEK-A-BOO 並木通り
東京都中央区銀座 5-4-9 ニューギンザ 5 ビル 4F
03・6254・5990

GINZA PEEK-A-BOO 中央通り
東京都中央区 2-6-16 ゼニア銀座ビル 10F
03・3562・8860

PEEK-A-BOO AVEDA 池袋東武
東京都豊島区西池袋 1-1-25 東武百貨店 池袋店 3F 11 番地
03・5928・0877

PEEK-A-BOO NEWoMan 新宿
東京都新宿区新宿 4-1-6 NEWoMan 新宿 4F
03・5361・6003
2016 年 3 月 25 日オープン

PEEK-A-BOO AVEDA アトレ恵比寿
2016 年春オープン

www.peek-a-boo.co.jp

COMPANY LIST

ANAP
03・3496・6768

株式会社アリミノ
03・3363・8211

株式会社コンフォートジャパン
0120・39・5410

株式会社ミルボン
0120・658・894

ケラスターゼ
sp.kerastase.jp

資生堂プロフェショナル株式会社
0120・81・4710

DEARTECK
0120・52・6022

FINE COSMETICS
03・3269・6621

SPECIAL THANKS

Fumio Kawashima　　Hiroshi Yazaki　　Takuyoshi Nishio　　Aya Yoshimi　　Momoko Iwasaki

TOKYO HAIR
最先端ヘアスタイルストーリー

2016年1月21日 初版第1刷発行

Staff

Design：Susumu Fujii
（Without P.100-111, 112-121 Souhei Nakamura）
Circulation：Aiko Miyata
Photo：Hikaru Funyu
（Without P.008-031 Shinji Serizawa, P.122-129 Shinpo Kimura）
Write：Misato Kikuchi（P.060-081, 082-093, 094–099, 122-129）
English Translation：Saori Ohara
Ilustration：Aimi Odawara
Edit：Junpei Ichikawa, Yuta Fukano

発行人　佐野裕
発行所　トランスワールドジャパン株式会社

〒150-0001
東京都渋谷区神宮前6-34-15 モンターナビル
Tel：03・5778・8599
Fax：03・5778・8743

印刷・製本 三松堂株式会社

Printed in Japan
©Transworld Japan Inc. 2016

本書の全部または一部を、著作権法で認められた範囲を超えて
無断で複写、複製、転載、あるいはデジタル化を禁じます。
乱丁・落丁本は小社送料負担にてお取替え致します。
ISBN 978-4-86256-172-5